WAKE UP TO YOUR HIGHER SELF

FROM ROBOTIC ACTION TO MINDFUL ENERGY

MORRIS J. COHEN

Order this book online at www.trafford.com
or email orders@trafford.com

Most Trafford titles are also available at major online book retailers.

Print information available on the last page.

ISBN: 978-1-4907-8334-5 (sc)
ISBN: 978-1-4907-8333-8 (e)

Trafford rev. 10/03/2017

 www.trafford.com

North America & international
toll-free: 1 888 232 4444 (USA & Canada)
fax: 812 355 4082

DEDICATION

To my family: Phyllis, Stephanie, Jeffrey, Larry, Shelley.
They are the people who make life worth living.

ACKNOWLEDGEMENTS

Many people contributed directly and indirectly to this book.

My wife, Phyllis, always encouraged me to write down all of my thoughts making up my philosophy of life that I have discussed with her over the many years she has put up with my "stuff".

My son, Jeffrey, with whom I have had many talks about the subjects in this book. He always brought to the table new and interesting ways of looking at life, and has greatly influenced my thinking.

My daughter, Stephanie, who has been and still is, a shining light of laughter, joy and happiness. Her smile and straight forwardness always brings warmth to my heart. She was directly responsible for introducing me to Sue Trumpfheller, who in turn introduced me to Martha Humphreys, my editorial consultant and Maria Albergato, the lady who is my consultant in developing a teaching program.

My son-in-law, Larry, who has been interested in my particular way of looking at life. He has shared his insights with me and our discussions clarified my intuitive understandings.

My educational consultant, Frances Heims, PhD who taught me how to organize my writing and was instrumental in teaching me how to amplify my concepts by asking the right questions.

My telephone friend, Sue Trumpfheller, who was extremely helpful in directing me to my editor and who gave me much needed information on the general subject of marketing, book publishing and other subjects pertinent to my project.

My editorial consultant and friend, Martha Humphreys, who has done a most professional job on editing my book and discussing various aspects of my concepts and philosophy in order to clarify them for our readers. She also introduced me to artist and educator Maria Albergato who is my consultant with regard to developing a teaching course.

My educational consultant, Maria Albergato, who has been most helpful in editing, text content and teaching course development. Maria created the cover art work and diagrams throughout the text. Maria is on the same wave length with me due to her years of meditation. Her insights and discussions have helped me tremendously.

My very good friend, Craig Marks, has been an inspiration to me. Our discussions about spirituality have been invaluable. His gentle and kind manner reflects how all human kind could be. I value him as a friend and as someone who understands where I am coming from. His editorial comments and organizational changes have made this book more user friendly and infinitely more effective.

My very good friend, Anne Marks, who is also a writer. Our discussions are always interesting and lively and she is willing to share her thoughts and ask questions which I find most unusual in this day and age. Our talks about writing motivated me to start this book.

My very good friend, Karen Allen PhD, who has always encouraged me in my work. Our philosophical discussions motivated me to think along new pathways. Her comments have enabled me to create a better product.

TABLE OF CONTENTS

ABOUT THE AUTHOR

Morris J. Cohen has been a successful businessman for over fifty years. He is the happily married father of two adult children. He has spent the past forty years in the study and practice of meditation, consciousness, and Eastern thought and philosophy. His study led him to the conception of personal programming. He has taught meditation for many years.

His studies in Eastern practices began with Transcendental Meditation and continued with workshops and seminars with Ken Keyes Jr., Jean Houston, and expert teachers of the Vipassana Meditation, Kripalu Yoga Center, Omega Institute, Princeton University, Silva Mind Control and Reiki.

His book "Wake Up To Your Higher Self...And Enjoy Life!" reflects his study of the works of J. Krishnamurti, Deepak Chopra, the Bhagavad Gītā, Hermann Hesse, Isaac Asimov, Ram Dass, His Holiness Maharishi Mahesh yogi, Herbert M. Shelton, Rudolph Steiner, Ernest Holmes, Thich Nhat Hanh and Mary Baker Eddy.

The author experienced a profound shift in perception, awareness and control of his experience of life, which so enhanced every aspect of his life that he decided to share his knowledge and understanding in the form of this book. He has dedicated himself to contributing the proceeds from this book and the forthcoming "Wake Up To Your Higher Self Workbook" to the education and support for the welfare of children in need.

FOREWORD

We are not our brains, bodies or personalities. These always change. The only anchor we have to reality is our true self. Instead of living in the fog of the external world of material "stuff", we must wake up in order to identify with our internal *mindful energy*. This will enable us to manage our external life in a truly creative, efficient, productive manner from the viewpoint of our true self.

It is difficult for most of us to believe in something that is hidden from our sight and yet is all around us and in every part of our brains and bodies. Everything in the universe was created by and is sustained by the unseen or spiritual or what I choose to call *mindful energy*. As *mindful energy* exists on a universal plane, it also exists individually within each of us. Our lives become easy and enriched once we access our personal piece of *mindful energy*.

Until then, people view external influences as the major element in their development and present existence. In addition to our waking, sleeping, and dreaming states, there is a fourth dimension. This dimension is *mindful energy*. This life force is all knowing; never changes; embodies love, beauty, truth, compassion, kindness, and above all, life itself. In order to evolve as human beings, we must make contact, communicate and become one with this force that is in reality our true self. In order to change our experience of life we need to rise above the automatic state we live in and enter the "knowing" state, where we realize that in essence we are pure consciousness.

True freedom means not to be subject to any of the desires of our egos and all their subsequent programming of our personalities.

All of our experience is subject to being filtered and altered by the programs created in our minds. Once we clear out the clutter of these programs so that the channel to our *mindful energy* can remain open at all times, we receive clear communication that will enrich and support our lives. We can escape the box that our programs have created for us and enjoy the freedom that is our birthright.

Much of our "rational mind" thinking is "irrational." In order to remedy this situation, we must learn to observe our thoughts in order to discriminate and refine these thoughts prior to taking action. It is a three step process: wake up, observe, and take charge. By instilling its own holistic, eternal personality in us in place of our ego-directed personality, our *mindful energy* provides the wisdom to achieve peace, pleasure and prosperity today, and every day in the future allowing us to manage our lives in an optimum manner.

Our true self is the source of all life, providing us with Instant Gratification now, in this moment, and for each moment after.

1

WAKING UP!

We live in an era of accelerated change, mass media, and instant communication. Our senses are bombarded nearly every waking moment. The truths that once anchored human beings have all but disappeared. Our society is built upon a materialistic economy that drives us to work harder and longer hours with little regard for our well-being. Aside from vacation, how often do we take time to go for quiet walks, lie in a hammock and look into the sky or our own souls, or leave behind the cell phone or laptop?

The majority of humankind experiences life through the filter of cultural and personal programs. These programs coupled with a concentration on the material stuff in our lives, clouds our internal perception and true self.

I am a self-made and successful businessman who took some time to tap into a source of consciousness and energy that I call *mindful energy*. I began to learn the art of meditation in an effort to enjoy the experience of life more and to alleviate a measure of business related stress. I didn't drop out of my family, circle of friends, or business life. I discovered the means of enhancing the experience of living. The process of meditation and internal reflection began to shift my perception and experience. That change permeated every aspect of my experience of life. Since meditating regularly, my thoughts seem to come from a different place.

The focus of my life shifted and the course of my thoughts, changed. I began to be more aware of my own thoughts and responses to them and to situations in which I found myself. Meditation put me in touch with a sense of knowing beyond my rational mind. It became the vehicle of finding my true self, peace of mind, and harmony. The experience has been so positive and energizing that I chose to share it with others. This book reflects the years I spent learning about meditation, consciousness, and Eastern thought and philosophy. It provides a detailed and easy to follow program and guide to wake up, observe, and act for the conscious experience of living.

Mindful Energy, Modern Man's Rosetta Stone

The Rosetta Stone, a stone slab found by a French soldier in 1799 near Rosetta, (Rashid, a town in N. United Arab Republic), bearing parallel inscriptions in Greek, Egyptian Hieroglyphics, and demotic characters made it possible for the translation of Ancient Egyptian Hieroglyphics and thereby the knowledge of that culture.

Modern man also has a Rosetta Stone. I call it *mindful energy* or the ability to know that we know with absolute certainty. This ability to "know that we know" allows us to translate the experience of our lives in order to discover our true self and have access to a lifetime of peace and prosperity beyond our imagination. Once we understand the effects of our thoughts, perceptions, feelings, emotions and programs of others on our essence, we can wake up to the reality of our existence.

That reality is not what we believe it to be:

- Your car is yours, but it is not you.
- Your house is yours, but it is not you.
- Your body is yours, but it is not you.

- Your thoughts are yours, but they are not you.
- Your personality is yours, but it is not you.
- The roles you play are yours, but they are not you.

Rather we are pure *mindful energy,* a non-material intelligent energy life force. Once mankind understands and accepts that knowledge, humanity will rise to new levels of being. When holistic humanity exists, each of us will allow our *mindful energy* to provide personal direction.

The first step in our evolution is to wake up to the reality of our existence. Consider the non-material element that allows us to experience our lives: "consciousness." Today, how aware are we of this element? Do we know how to best utilize it? Are we conscious, but totally unconscious of being conscious? At best we use our five senses, and, therefore, are able to be conscious to the extent of those five senses. What could we become if we become more aware of this fundamental Block of Pure Consciousness, which I call *mindful energy*?

We are on "automatic" and not even aware of it. Our senses bring input into our brains, our minds "think" and create programs and we "re-act" to life through the "programs" our minds are creating. Is this all there is to being conscious?

The way in which we experience our life is through the medium of thought programming. The outside events or situations are secondary to this experience, and have no direct bearing on our experience. Our thought filters interpret our experience, i.e., whether we are happy, sad, or anywhere in between.

Your life can become an exercise of "Choosing to Act" rather than "Re-Acting" to events, situations and people. Using the *mindful energy* available to all of us, each of us needs to release and expand our special talent to serve humanity and ourselves. I believe it is incumbent upon all of us to make our appearance on earth the richest that it can be, so that each life will serve as a beacon to others in the present, and to those who will follow us in the future.

Mankind needs to serve Mankind.

What Will This Book Do For You?

You will learn how to motivate yourself to become master of your experiences, thoughts and emotions. You will recognize that you can be in charge of creating a better experience of your life even if your external situation remains the same. You will also have more energy to change the situations in which you find yourself, because you will not waste your energy in useless negative emotions that can drain you physically and create ill health in your body and mind. You will find methods to teach yourself "to get out of the box", the restrictive space in which you live your life.

The "Wake Up To Your Higher Self" workbook is designed to reinforce your learning and enhance your efforts to reach your goals. It will ease the new process into your consciousness, allowing it to change your life: your thinking, your actions, your emotions and your reactions to what is going on around you. It will make you much more aware of what happens, and help you to examine why events and feelings take place, and suggest remedies for previous inappropriate behaviors and feelings. Yes, you can control and do something about your life and the ways you experience it.

Until now, you have been an actor on the stage of your life. From now on, you can be the writer, producer, director, actor and audience in your own movie. You can choose your own scripts instead of accepting the story line that is being fed to you. Your life can be experienced in its totality, and as it relates to every one else on the planet. In addition, you experience the excitement for living each and every moment to its fullest. It will allow you to re-define your "work" and your "fun". Perhaps the best result of this concept allows you to achieve the greatest integration into "oneness"–that state of mind of being at one with the world and with oneself regardless of any outside forces.

It is not as complicated as it sounds: How often have you simply "known" something without having any reason to know it? This is the experience of tuning into to this *mindful energy* without realizing you are doing so.

Man invented radio and television which relays information to and from receiving and sending stations. So, too, your brain may be capable of this type of communication without you being aware of it. When you are aware of these relationships you can, in turn, tune into the vast sending station that exists in a higher dimension or dimensions that exist all around you. By doing so you can see the "wholeness" of life and the universe and gain the knowledge to change yourself and your society into a more evolved, loving and moral state of being. That is our goal for you, and you will be part of your own metamorphosis.

Think of a human being as a computer. The power may be on, but the RAM is using only a fraction of its available memory. The computer's actions occur in the present, but could create events in the future. The computer's actions are the result of software programs, but the hardware remains the same. Our actions, too, are a result of the programs we learned, but our hardware remains the same. *mindful energy* is the operating system. Windows, DOS or Linux, supplies the language for the computer to function, *mindful energy* provides the information for the human being to fulfill his or her destiny. All that is required of us to learn our system is to pay attention.

Let me show you the way to "take charge" of your minute to minute experience of your life. You can enjoy the experience of your life as never before and have the added benefit of more energy, creativity, health and productivity.

GOALS OF THIS BOOK

- You can work toward getting what you want, while simultaneously being happy with what you have.
- You can control the way you experience your life and the forces that impinge upon it.
- You have the choice of experiencing what happens as enjoyable or unpleasant, or you can choose a place somewhere between these two poles.
- Knowledge and action can take you to your highest levels of self-actualization, intellectual essence, and the highest level of awareness.
- You will reach a place of intense peacefulness and perfection where every atom of your body and mind knows that everything that has happened, is happening, and will happen is the way it should be.
- You can be secure, have elevating experiences, and participate in the joy of love.
- The true essence of your being is pure consciousness; i.e. an empty plate on which all types of food can be presented. The "plate" (consciousness) can be washed clean and a different "food" (experience) can be placed on it on a moment-to-moment basis.
- You are in a constant state of evolution. You can choose to drive around in first gear or you can accelerate to overdrive or superdrive.
- The feeling of a constant source of love is within yourself.
- As you reach into yourself for answers to your life today, you will be able to apply this knowledge toward understanding

those around you.

- Replace ego-driven programs with harmonious, peaceful programs.
- Knowing that you know: peaceful serenity, acceptance of what is.
- You will evolve at your own speed.

HOW YOU WILL ACHIEVE THESE GOALS

You Will Learn to:

- Raise your level of consciousness in all areas of your life.
- Change your life: your thinking, your actions, and your emotions.
- Assess your reactions to what is going on around you.
- Examine why events and feelings take place.
- Remedy previous inappropriate behaviors and feelings.
- Take control of the ways you experience your life and act on your experiences.
- Recognize the sequences of feelings, actions, and thoughts that control your life.
- Eliminate robotic functioning and teach yourself to choose your own feelings and behaviors. Then consciously decide to act.
- Motivate yourself to become master of your experiences (physical, emotional, social, and intellectual) (PESI).
- Recognize that you can be in charge of creating a better experience of your life even if your external situation remains the same.
- Have more energy to change.
- Ensure your energies are not being wasted in useless negative emotions that can drain you physically and create ill health in your body and mind.
- Find methods to teach yourself to "get out of the box"—that

space that dictates behavior to you—so that you are in charge of
the whole project of your life!

- Learn to reinforce your positive learning.
- "Know that you know" in your physical, mental, and
  emotional realm.

Note in the diagram below that the reactive you, surrounded
by your current thoughts, emotions, and experiences will begin to
change as you read the text and complete the exercises in the text and
the workbook. You will begin to experience a new way of knowing
and use *mindful energy* to direct your life. Increasingly, you will live
your life directed from the *true conscious* self which is *mindful energy.*

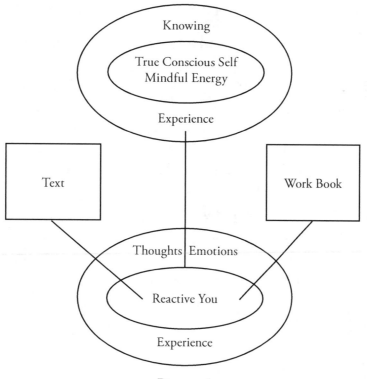

Diagram 1

2

CONSCIOUSNESS

What Is Your Goal in Becoming More Aware?

The goal of the process of becoming aware is to identify and explore your robotic behaviors, actions, and reactions–to progress from the robotic to the objective, observing, and awareness level. As you climb toward your highest awareness level, you become acutely aware of your programs so that you can recognize them as they appear in your daily life's situations and change them based on your objective observation of them.

'Consciousness', or the awareness of our existence in time and place, is the setting within which all of our life's experiences occur. Think of it as the envelope containing all of our thoughts and experiences. Most of us do not realize the importance of this element, and we experience it without being fully aware of it.

There are four levels of consciousness:

- Waking
- Sleeping
- Dreaming
- Knowing (*mindful energy*)

All of us have experienced the first three levels, but few have accessed the fourth level.

As soon as our awareness includes *mindful energy* we can use it with our mental programs to create peace of mind, creativity, effectiveness, and anything else that leads to our evolution as human beings.

This chapter will develop your understanding of this fourth level.

The fourth level can be experienced through meditation, which is "rising above the thought level." This fourth level observes and is capable of changing and enhancing our experience of life. It guides us to the realization of our "true self." In other words, it is *mindful energy* leading us to the realization that in essence, we are *"mindful energy."*

Don't let the term "meditation" intimidate you, for there are as many forms of meditation as there are people who practice it. For our purposes, meditation can be defined as: observation of your present circumstance. Instead of some esoteric practice, meditation becomes accessible and achievable by anyone who seeks a deeper understanding of their present reality. The practice of meditation allows you to experience the serene contemplation of living every moment of your life.

If you are alive, you experience change. Every cell in your body changes from moment to moment, instant to instant, second to second. Change is always with us, and yet we need an anchor to stabilize our existence in our world of constant change. Through meditation you can access the *mindful energy* residing within you, and through that realize your true identity and take charge of your future. We must be flexible in order to see the opportunity inherent in each moment. *Mindful energy* is the answer.

"Knowing" is the awareness that you are observing your thoughts (i.e., listening), emotions (i.e., feelings), and actions (i.e., watching) as if you were watching a movie and being aware you are watching a movie, without identifying with the characters in the movie. Knowingness is pure consciousness without thoughts. For instance, consider your mind the screen onto which the movie is projected prior to the film starting, it is that rarified state you can attain when you have risen above your active thought processes and look down on them peacefully, objectively, and with a sense of "just being". This state of mind enables you to observe all that is happening wherever you are without conflicted, inappropriate feelings, behaviors, and thoughts that occupy the lives of most of us. There is a sense or presence of peace that permeates your very being. You benefit from a sense of confidence that you can handle any situation without fear or insecurity.

If you can isolate your thoughts into concrete units, there is always a pause, a space between each of them. That space, the "gap" between the thoughts is your higher form of intelligence that exists prior to any thoughts being formed. That superior consciousness knows everything. That "pure consciousness" residing within you cannot bring its light of love to your surface consciousness until you clear the path by eliminating the useless clutter of unsupervised thinking. The messy mind bars your *mindful energy* residing within.

Think about watching a movie and getting so emotionally involved that you lose yourself in it. Your body reacts; your heart beats faster, your breathing rate increases, and tension tightens your muscles. You associate these reactions with feelings stemming from the characters involved in its plot. When you activate the aware state of mind you can still identify completely with the characters in the movie. You feel the same emotions, think the same thoughts, etc. while simultaneously observing yourself doing all of the above. In fact, the entire experience is enhanced because you are aware of being aware. You experience a different type of pleasure when you remain in the aware state of mind. You can watch the same movie in the "knowing" state and enjoy it with serenity without identifying completely with the characters–understanding them, enjoying them, but not identifying with them. You can observe the deeper aspects of the movie, such as cause and effect, structures of light and dark, how background music heightens the action, how the movie is affecting you and why. You enjoy a higher order of learning and joyfulness available from your higher level of consciousness.

When you watch a movie, do you feel that the actor IS the character he/she is playing (portraying)? The better the actor, the more real it seems to be. However, the actor on the stage realizes it is only an act and that is why he enjoys acting. He can immerse himself in the part. In addition, when the play is over, he can step out of his role and become himself again. Do you think that some actors like acting because they can assume roles and get away from their negative perceptions of themselves? Do they "lose themselves in the whole experience? It may be an escape act for some of them or they may be more proficient in utilizing their inner intelligence to view their newfound character in order to enhance their acting.

If you are so caught up in the experience of the movie, you may become upset. But if you are *aware* that you are "watching" the movie, you can appreciate the acting and story without that feeling. Furthermore, if you are fully aware, you can be fully conscious and spontaneous at the same time. Actors, too, can be fully aware of their cues, but if they are also spontaneous, their acting becomes more believable.

There is no change in emotional levels produced by the programmed mind unless *you* choose to change the levels. In effect, you can have complete control.

Your programmed mind, if left to its own devices, will not allow you to live at the optimal level of consciousness as it prevents you from being a more conscious person. It is possible that you are only conscious enough to exist, without the pleasures that you can experience from a higher level of awareness. Certain programs dictate behavior, which is not always in our best interest. The will, intuition and power inherent in the *mindful energy* is automatically toward peace, harmony and love. The will inherent in our "rational mind" is toward material or ego-driven, which is quite the opposite.

What Relationship Exists Between Consciousness and Your Body?

Most people think that consciousness and their bodies are one. They are not aware that consciousness is separate from their physical selves. In India, a yogi can reduce his heartbeat to a bare fraction of that in his everyday life. He can lie on a bed of nails and feel no pain. So it is that the body can be at the will of your mind if you so choose.

Where Does the Mind Fit Into this Equation?

The four areas of mindful energy, mind, mental, and physical are then allowed to mix. Mindful energy allows its qualities into our programmed mind. The mind then re-organizes the brain to conform to these qualities, which are then translated into the mental and physical realms and manifests itself in your body's actions, thoughts, programs, emotions, and feelings.

How Can My Mind Affect My Physical Self?

I started jogging on the beach. I opened all the channels to my spiritual self, and I allowed the flow of mindful energy to enter my mind. In turn, this led my body to function effortlessly without getting tired or out of breath. This took place even though I had not been jogging regularly and, therefore, my body was not in condition. It was as if my body immediately went into a conditioned phase. The chaos of the world around me was suddenly stilled by the infinite peacefulness that flowed through me.

How Do Reflections Enter the Process?

The mirror of reality depends on the quality of stillness your mind happens to be in. When no waves exist on the clear surface of the pond, then the reflection can be seen all the way to the depths of the pond, just as it really is. When waves are created, then the view from the depths is obscured. The reflection of the sky, trees, birds, in the water is only that–a reflection. They are distorted by the waves on the water. They are not seen for what they really are. If the water is your spirit, then you must have a clear mind in order for your spirit to become a catalyst for your growth. Happiness and sorrow are but ripples on the surfaces of the pond. Peacefulness is the narrow band that connects both elements. Peacefulness is the quality of the spirit. In any situation you can use the reflection of the outer material world (that includes your body, its functioning, your rational mind and its thought) to reflect upon the surface of your spiritual being. The clarity of this reflection depends upon your peace of mind. If there are no winds stirring up the outer surface of your mind, then you can view events and situations in that holistic place where the whole unfolding tapestry of life itself occurs.

How Do You Become Aware of Your Feelings, Thoughts, and Behaviors?

The main vehicle is meditation–both active (dual tracking) and passive meditation. One form of active meditation is the written or audio recording of your minute-to-minute thoughts, feelings (physical), emotions, and cause and effect reflections of your thoughts and actions. Read the written record out loud to yourself with as much awareness as possible and realize these thoughts are not you. Regarding the audio recording, listen to your thoughts and realize they are not you. Passive meditation accesses the pure consciousness which resides within you. Your everyday experience is a combination of the *mindful energy* of which you are probably unaware, and the programming which activates your daily life. The clean plate of your *mindful energy* has remnants of former meals which must be rinsed off in order to live your fullest life. Accessing the *mindful energy* allows you to create your own reality, and your experience of life, even with the same external set of circumstances.

ACTIVITY

Think of a negative feeling that you have had in the past. Identify it, and describe it emotionally and physically.

Now ask yourself what preceded the negative emotion. You can then begin to understand the programming that resulted in the emotion you described. This programming was put into your "software" when you were young, but now your conscious self[1] can change that. An example may be a sense of insecurity that was drilled into you from many sources. The emotion you feel may be of despair, frustration,

[1] "conscious self" = mindful energy = knowing state

and self doubt, unwillingness to try new things, or even taking charge of your decision making process. These negative events can impact you physically as well as emotionally. Your body may not be able to handle the situation, so you wind up with psychosomatic symptoms that help you to temporarily avoid facing the situation and yourself realistically. Once you take charge you can feel good physically as well as emotionally and mentally. When you look at your previous life from a higher vantage point—that of peaceful pure consciousness or awareness, your earlier hang-ups disappear.

How Can You Change the Experience You are Having?

You can create your own reality in full conscious awareness. For example, when you are on a vacation, do you feel yourself changing into another person—still doing things, but with no stress attached, no sense of urgency, no need to get it "done?" What level of consciousness do you think you have attained? Is it more relaxing, tension-free, filled with joy and exhilaration at "just being?" This is programming that relates to "vacation." At work it is exactly the opposite. Why? Because of the programming in your brain—programming that creates stress at work and relaxation on vacation.

When you participate in a sport, you can become physically tired. The thoughts in your mind tell you that you are tired. You feel mentally and emotionally tired because you are "thinking" of being tired. However, if you get out of your thoughts and watch your body being tired, your body will not feel tired any longer. The reason is that thinking translates into bodily sensations. Therefore, do not think about being tired, and you won't be "tired." You can associate certain physical feelings with "being tired." Instead of feeling the feelings, observe them and watch what happens.

The objective is to be "objective" in all aspects of your life. Do not allow your thoughts to run your life. Your thoughts should act as a friend and secretary reminding you of options, appointments, responsibilities, etc.–not as a "dictator" of your feelings and actions. When a thought places a negative value on a situation, it is only because of a past program. You have learned to think and act negatively as well as positively. With awareness, you can discard the negativity in your programming and begin anew with positivism.

Consider this: You cannot see the whole from inside the box of your consciousness. Once you move yourself outside of the confines of your current consciousness into the open sea of *mindful energy* surrounding you, you are motivated to be more fully aware. *Mindful energy* is the repository for all possible energy and serenity.

Your life may seem futile and unimportant because of your limited vision. Your life expands by moving into your higher level of consciousness or awareness where you can begin to see clearly. *Mindful energy* is the pure essence of awareness within you.

All material matter manifests itself from this pure space. The result can be a higher level of performance, action, behavior, or thought. Not operating at this level of higher consciousness results in failure to attain the full potential that resides in you. When you learn to understand and use this awareness level for the good of mankind, you will have evolved as a higher being to the next level of creation. That is your destiny.

How Can I Determine Whether I am in an Automatic Mode or in a Mode of Conscious Awareness?

When you meditate on a consistent basis, you will step into the "awareness" zone. This can only be done by experiencing; i.e., you cannot describe a color or a smell without the actual experience. However, physically doing certain exercises may speed up the experiential process such as recording and playing back your thoughts or writing them down first and then reading them out loud to yourself.

ACTIVITY

Write down one feeling you had earlier today. Describe it briefly.

_____

_____

_____

Below are two columns labeled "automatic" and "conscious awareness." Record feelings in each column based on "automatic" and "conscious awareness."

Automatic	Conscious Awareness

Total: _____   Total: _____

Now add up the number of feelings from each column. Are there more in column 1 or 2? What process do you think you are using more–"automatic" or "conscious awareness?" Tell why you found more in one column than the other.

_____

_____

_____

Now that you have explored feeling in some depth, try this.

Write down how you really wanted to feel. Determine for yourself whether more particulars of your desired feeling were "automatic" or "being consciously aware" by putting an "X" before each "automatic" feeling, and a "Y" before each "aware" feeling.

_____

_____

_____

_____

_____

_____

Let's take this line of thinking further.

Identify and describe one activity you have been doing for a long time.

_____

_____

_____

_____

_____

Examine it closely. Decide:

- What behaviors, feelings, and actions were involved?
- Were your actions automatic, or observant and objective?
- Were you using your higher consciousness?
- Why? Why not?

When you function in your higher consciousness, your level of joy increases, you can evaluate your actions from that space above thought, and you can unburden yourself of useless, non-productive thoughts (programming).

SUMMARY- UNDERSTANDING CONSCIOUSNESS

- The true essence of your being is pure consciousness, i.e. an empty plate on which all types of food can be presented. The "plate" (consciousness) can be washed clean and a different "food" (experience) can be placed on it on a moment to moment basis.

- Knowing you are pure consciousness, you can unburden yourself from past, inappropriate thoughts, feelings, and actions, leaving you more time and energy to spend on the present to objectively examine situations.
- Life is a series of conscious and unconscious feelings, attitudes and behaviors.
- Your presence here on earth has a purpose.
- You can function and be happiest by being a part of, and apart from the reality of the moment.

3

EXPERIENCING

How To Observe Everyday Experiences From A Different Standpoint And To See Experiences More Objectively

Experience differs from consciousness because it requires action. To experience something requires active participation in events or activities. We accumulate knowledge and skill from our experiences. How we perceive the experience determines our assessment of it. The same experience will have different value for each person participating in it. For most of us, our experience of life is determined by our programs. The instructions given to us or observed by us as to how to behave in certain circumstances are the programs our parents, caregivers and society provided us from birth. Those programs determine how we interpret our experience and to a large extent dictate our reactions. As you accumulate experiences, they have consequences for determining how and why you do things.

For our purposes, experience is not restricted to events, but can include people with whom we interact. For people you meet can influence your state of mind by their state of mind, their vibrations.

Therefore you feel differently with different people. Or you may experience the same person differently depending on their current internal activity. You notice differences in their tone of voice, their use of words, and their body language because of the influences of their inner state when interacting with you. The same words may come out of two different mouths, but you receive the message in totally different ways because of your belief or trust in one person as opposed to your negative feelings about the other.

Experiences can also create a yo-yo effect—swinging you from one state to another, because you do not evaluate your experiences within you. By taking the time to objectively observe, and then evaluate your experiences, you can use your consciousness to improve your life. Since your experiences affect your health, physiological functioning, analytical functioning, your creativity, your social behavior, your productivity, peacefulness, and your overall outlook on life, it makes sense to create positive results from all of them.

Experience results in emotional reactions. Recognize that your feelings can give you signals if you are aware of them. And those feelings are experiences in and of themselves. Our consciousness allows us to observe the feelings and evaluate them when we access the pure consciousness of *mindful energy*.

The process involved in experiencing and then acting is important for you to experience objectively. As you go through life, you create and embrace some experiences and avoid others. You recognize different experiences because of the interactions of programs you established yourself and those that were established by those around you. The result is a combination of internal and external programming. Consider this: You need to experience and rationalize. You can read about golf but you don't "know" it until you play the game.

People can react in totally different ways to the same scenario "out there." For instance, the next time you attend a meeting where the same information is given to the participants, observe their faces, body motions, and the verbal behaviors they engage in. Do they continue it after the meeting? Do some act and react more angrily than others? Each person's perceptions (programs) will make him feel and behave differently. He may have totally ignored "facts," he may have been influenced by his active dislike of the speaker, or he may have his own agenda that prohibits his rational appraisal of the objective situation and the information provided.

Perhaps the finest experience available to human beings is love. Even love has its own language lying within. You may have to dig for it, but the gold you find is priceless.

In the following exercises, let's look at some experiences in your life to determine whether or not they have served you well. Think about whether or not you would like to repeat them. How much does your answer result from the experience or your perception of it?

ACTIVITY

List ten situations you now find yourself engaged in on a regular basis on a sheet of paper, e.g. note how you experience each situation. Then list ten experiences you would like to have (using the same situations). Is the list of experiences you now have different from those you would like to have? How? Why do you think they are different? Were the experiences on your first list programmed by others, generated by your own choice, or actually a combination of both? Can you now say that more of those experiences you would like to have come from within yourself rather than their having been imposed on you? Have you been wagging your tail or have outside forces wagged it for you? Look at your list of experiences again. Think about why you would like to have those experiences. As you become more aware of your emotions and feelings in the experiencing of your behaviors know that you (automatically) know with your five senses of feeling, touching, hearing, seeing, and smelling. Tune into your 6th sense– that of awareness of the other five senses–and **KNOW THAT YOU KNOW** what the other five senses are all about. That way, you can truly experience what is being experienced. Feel your experience, but "know" you are feeling it. You "know" that you "know."

ACTIVITY

Keep a journal to make you more aware of your role and that of others in your everyday work and pleasure. Explore different scenarios and write down the different feelings you are having. Include the involvement of your five senses. When you have thought about your experiences, you can better work on observing and correcting your programs when necessary. You can now concentrate on "how do I feel?"–not what is "correct thinking." The first sign comes with feeling. In that way, you begin to concentrate on changing your life space and the experiences that occur within it. Do I feel peaceful, loving, harmonious or angry, irritated, annoyed?

ACTIVITY

Take 10 minutes to write down some things you desire. Write down everything your mind is telling you and the emotions that you are feeling. Do not attempt to interpret or edit your thoughts or emotions. Write them down exactly as you think and express them. Write how your body is reacting to your thoughts and how your energy level reacts.

How Does Desire Relate To Your Motivation?

Our programs are created both internally and externally, although their evolution, operation, and results may be intertwined (intuition/ genetics). At birth we are the clean plate upon which our caretakers, friends and family place **their** choice of foods. Our reaction to a specific "food" can internally change the program, or create a desire to explore a different cuisine.

For instance: your father is a deep sea fisherman and you accompanied him on many fishing trips. On those trips you noticed the dolphins following the boat, so you decide that you want to be an explorer of the undersea world of dolphins. First, you have the desire to do this, and then you figure out the ways to get you there. You decide to go to college, perhaps even graduate school, apply for an internship on a Jacque Cousteau expedition, and begin your own research on your area of particular interest.

But let's backtrack for a moment. Where did you learn about dolphins and the sea in the first place? What made you choose this career above all others? Could your program have led to your writing fiction about dolphins or concentrating on their migration paths rather than studying their genetic makeup? You may even have selected this activity on a whim because you felt that nothing you chose was so important so you might as well do something different. The programs of today have emanated from your past. Your childhood may have been spent in a coastal village where you got your love for the sea and its inhabitants. Conversely, you may have been raised in a crowded slum in the heart of a rundown city and your greatest desire was to remove yourself from that environment as productively as possible. But did you push yourself, or was someone else pulling you? Or is your ambition a combination of factors both internal and external?

Where Does Objective and Subjective Reality Fit in?

Most people do not connect the dots between their "inner" and "outer" selves. Their representation of themselves and those they meet–even the experiences they have–is one-sided, unidimensional, or from just one point of view. They are unaware of the influences of inner and outer programming from their pasts because they may not even know about the existence of their programs. Therefore, they are stuck at a rather primitive level of functioning that limits their capacity to understand themselves, others, and the world around them. But, most importantly, they really know nothing about themselves–their real desires, the way they function, the true essence of their being, and their purpose here on earth. They have not learned to look at their lives objectively. Only then can they approach true reality.

How Do You Objectively Explore Reality?

Reality is viewed through a clear mind. However, you experience the world, yourself, and all the situations you encounter subjectively. What happens outside your head really does not matter because you are creating the emotional experience of each moment within yourself.

You are the creator–you choose your own reality. The mere fact that you choose to explore a situation, takes it immediately from the realm of objectivity to the arena of your mind where it is subjective. The decision alone requires that you separate out "objective reality." All reality, therefore, is subjective. Your subjective reality is based on past and present programming. You even select those things you want to explore and leave out others, thus compounding the situation. You cannot be in total control of objective reality. However, exploring subjective reality can be a road toward attaining a measure of objectivity. There is the possibility of retaining a clear mind (without thought) and thus experiencing the entire material world objectively, through the eyes of your *mindful energy*. All your "programming" will then emanate from your true self, i.e. your spiritual being.

What Barriers Are There When Trying to Attain Objective Reality?

Your ego can sometimes get in the way. Your ego's programs are totally subjective, self-enhancing, and protective. But protective of what? The ego is the repository of all those programs that make you feel important, rich, in control, respected, admired, or a combination of other beliefs, feelings, and subsequent behaviors. When you recognize and accept the destructive powers of your ego, you switch to a higher state of awareness and objectivity where you can create your own reality consciously rather than unconsciously. Some examples may clarify this.

In the Japanese film, *Rashamon*, an incident occurs which is viewed by several people. However, the same incident is viewed differently by each observer because each character perceives the incident from his subjective vantage point–his own point of view.

What is happening within the different characters is the result of each character's "reality"–really his or her subjective evaluation of the events taking place. So each one perceives the whole differently. Another picture, *Life Is Beautiful,* takes place during World War II. An Italian man and his young son are sent to a concentration camp where conditions deteriorate daily. He releases his previous life's programs that sustained his ego, then engages in deliberately bizarre actions to protect his child. He appraised the situation as objectively as he could, and learned to act in his son's best interest. He created a *subjective reality* for his son that ultimately resulted in his own death, but saved his son's life.

On a lighter note, recall when you played a good golf game and you were unhappy? You wanted a lower score, or a problem at home was distracting you, or you had just purchased a new club and expected better results. Any one of those factors clouded your experience. Yet someone else came in with the same score and was happy. Your experience was a result of what is going on in your brain, and therefore you directed it. You can change your experience, by accessing your *mindful energy,* which will create a different result. The disappointment you felt may have been the result of inappropriate, outdated programs lingering from your past. It is possible to redirect your feelings and actions in all aspects of your life.

Subjective and Objective Reality

Some people think that they are functioning optimally when they get in the "zone"; a state of intensely focused perception to the exclusion of all other internal and external stimuli. They may know they are in a different place, but they don't know how they got there and may not be able to replicate the experience. Our process requires that you rise above the zone to a level where you can watch yourself being in the zone and you know you are watching yourself operating in this zone. A lawyer can be totally immersed—and even have a feeling of being "lost" in writing his brief. *Now you can do the same thing but, in addition, be totally aware of what you are doing.* You are the ultimate observer. This extra—and final—step is important because you realize that you have been mostly unconscious of your experience of life.

On one level, you can see, hear, feel, taste and smell, so you think you are conscious. Only when you rise above the thinking level, do you realize how unconscious you have been all your life. For example, if you are rendered unconscious by a fall; only when you awake do you realize you have been unconscious. Reaching this higher level is important because all of your thinking and feeling and understanding are now understandable and capable of being directed for the benefit of mankind. Relationships and understanding other people reach a new level. You also realize that "consciousness," the element we all utilize every moment, is not materially connected to our bodies or minds. It is in reality our true *mindful energy,* which inhabits our body/mind vehicle for a time. There are many levels through which it travels and our lifetime is but one of these trips. This realization alters our perception of life and why we are here in a quite dramatic sense. This leads us to begin the process of utilizing "consciousness" at other levels.

Is Objective Reality More Important Than Subjective Reality?

Your objective is to be as "objective" as possible as you examine all the aspects of your life. Your unbiased, objectively observed thoughts, actions, and feelings can act as friend and secretary reminding you of options, appointments, and responsibilities. But the danger lies in the thought itself. Do not allow biased, embedded, unexamined thoughts to run your life as a "dictator" of your feelings and actions. Just thinking and saying, "I will be objective. I will not let previous experiences mar my objective examination of the 'facts'" will start you on your journey. Let this be the beginning of programming yourself (yes, this is a program!) to be constantly alert to what is going on around and inside you physically, emotionally, socially, and intellectually. The next step is that of learning how to observe–objectively!

Start to realize that you are acting out your own programs, and recognize that you do not have to be trapped within the script of your past programs which lead to negative emotions. As you observe the cause/effect relationship of your inner programming and the effect it has on your emotional experience of the situation, you will realize that it is your inner program and not the outer event, situation, or person that creates your particular experience of the act or situation at that particular time. You can facilitate good observation by concentrating on your actions, thoughts, and feelings. Start by examining simple actions. When you raise a glass of water to your lips, say, "I know I am raising a glass to my lips." Do the same for your thoughts and feelings. Begin to observe how you think, act, and emote. Become more aware of your programmed existence.

ACTIVITY

Recall an embarrassing social situation you found yourself in. Write down your observations about the way you reacted in that specific social situation. Do you like the way you reacted? Why? Be an *observer* of yourself and others. Is there any thing you would like to change in your way of feelings, thinking, reacting, behaving, and seeing, etc.? Why?

_____

_____

_____

_____

What Can Affect the Process of Observation?

Internal and external forces constantly impinge on your conscious and unconscious self. They can be positive or negative, and can alter your programming at any moment. Your past programming may be telling you: Do not change anything; things should remain as they are; change can bring unknown threats. The key here is that *change is a constant!* The only element that does not change is "consciousness" itself. When you rise above your thoughts and enter the realm of "no change," it becomes a stabilizing force. It is a safe platform from which you can see yourself and all others you come into contact with. Being in this "safe" place enables you to respond to life's situations in an optimum manner, without fear.

After you become more intimately acquainted with your "safe" place, you will realize that this realm has more to offer you than just being a 'safe' haven. There is infinite intelligence, wisdom, power, and creativity locked up within its walls. And all this is available to you if you persevere and remain there long enough to find its riches.

Have you watched and listened to testimony at a trial on TV? Have you noticed the differences in the ways different witnesses describe an incident, people's behavior, the clothing they were wearing, the distance away from the scene the person mentioned, even the timing of the incident? Observation can be distorted by attitude, poor vision or hearing, and so many other factors. The movie, *Twelve Angry Men* dramatizes the roles of the prosecution, defense, and the jurors in particular, and how circumstances can change in an instant. It is up to you as a good researcher to evaluate the things you have heard, read or seen. Apply vigorous methods of analysis so that you will arrive at a truthful conclusion based on all the evidence.

ACTIVITY

Observe and write out just one thing that you desire. Write down what you want to happen or not happen and ask yourself if you can live without its being fulfilled. Once you begin to *observe* your thoughts, behavior, and emotions, you can begin to discern the programs that you were operating under–those that you programmed yourself and those that controlled you. Who was in charge (was it your program)? Who do you want to be in charge? Your *mindful energy*. The more time you spend in this higher state of awareness, the more control you can have over the ultimate quality of your life.

Start to realize that you are acting out your own scripts or programs. Start to realize that you are not trapped within the scripts of your past inappropriate emotions. As you keep observing the cause/effect relationship of your inner programming and the effect it has on your emotional experience of the situation, you will realize that it is your inner program and not the outer event, situation, or person that creates your particular experiencing of the act or situation at that particular time. Your inner program creates your reactions to the situation and a cycle of cause-and-effect begins. You must "choose to act" in lieu of "reacting."

SUMMARY: UNDERSTANDING EXPERIENCES

About Experiencing Life

- There are many ways to experience what is going on in your life and in the lives of others.
- This experiencing has consequences for determining how and why you do things.
- People you meet can influence your state of mind by their mental vibrations, i.e., their state of mind.
- You feel differently with different people.
- Messages sent and received in various forms affect the ways life is experienced.
- People's inner workings affect their ways of experiencing life.
- Experiences result in behavior, feeling, and attitude change.
- You can optimize your experiences within you.
- Your experience level can affect your health, physiological functioning, analytical functioning, your creativity, your social behavior, your productivity, peacefulness, and your overall outlook on life.
- Feelings can become stronger when experiencing life more fully.
- Objectivity is necessary in examining your experiences.
- Your experiences of life are the result of interactions of programs you established yourself and those that were established by those around you.
- You can read about life but you don't own it until you actually

experience it.

- You may be experiencing life from the narrow perspective of your own personal programs that were established long ago.
- You can let your programs operate you, or you can direct them at a highly conscious, aware level.
- You can live within a framework or box of your own creation, and not be aware of how it all happened.
- You can learn to place your life onto a global, universal, and all encompassing field that will enhance and broaden your life as you go beyond your individualistic mode.
- You can utilize your innate *mindful energy* to run and direct your thoughts.
- Programming can create your experiences.
- Experiences can turn into a program.
- Your experiences and your programs can be interactive.
- You ignored some experiences, took parts from others, or perhaps even took an entire experience into yourself.
- During this process, you may have put more weight on some information.
- You may have interpreted it both subjectively and objectively.
- You were programmed to respond positively to some experiences and information and negatively to others.
- Experiences can create total programs almost immediately.
- They can totally destroy various pleasurable parts of previously established set of behaviors, feelings, and expectations.
- You may be unable to dissect the cause of present behavior and separate out the bad part that destroyed enjoyable experiences.

4

THOUGHT

The dictionary refers to "thought" as the product of mental activity; that which one thinks; the process of thinking; any conception existing in the mind as a result of mental understanding, awareness, or activity. You can create a better product by accessing *mindful energy* and bypassing the usual "thinking process".

In this chapter you will learn that thoughts are "thinking" you. Instead of you (*mindful energy*) being the director of your thinking process, i.e. listening to these thoughts emanating from your brain and observing how you feel emotionally and physically and then objectively making decisions as to how to handle these thoughts.

The usual process is that other "older thought" programs make decisions on the newer thoughts. You think "you" are making these decisions, but until you can raise your awareness to listen and observe from outside the box of your thoughts, "you" (the true self) are outside the loop and not making these decisions.

What is Thought?

Thought is the steering wheel of your mind. The steering wheel of your car guides the vehicle on its journey. The vehicle can follow your directions, or could drive on a route suggested by some one else. In either case, your thoughts can be objective; but you are governed by your programs much of the time, which results in your thinking subjectively, or less rationally. Sadly, that could be the be all and end all of your existence. You might never rise above your thoughts to access your *mindful energy*. But once you do that, you can take charge of your thoughts. You can "choose to act" rather than simply react according to your old programmed responses that are based on faulty thought processes. Intellectually, every thought should be perceived as an objective thought, but earlier programs create in you subjective, personal thoughts. These personal thoughts have to be assessed to determine their value to you in allowing you to experience life's events most fully.

Your consciousness should be "awake" while your thought process is working. My interpretation is <u>not</u> to actively evaluate, rather allow the mind to do its evaluation and let the answer emerge without "actively" thinking. With less energy expended, it is much easier. The results come from an integration of your higher self utilizing the data your brain has collected. Give your brain instructions to evaluate and let it go; the answers will come.

To retrieve the information you seek, release the steering wheel and allow your *mindful energy* to drive you home.

The Process of Thought.

Thought is generally viewed as one idea–a thought–or as a process–thinking whereby you apply reason and, hopefully, measured evaluation, to your ideas, emotions, and actions. Your thinking skills have evolved over time, and you may have developed "objectivity" in appraising all that surrounds you and operates within yourself.

Thoughts can be simple or complex; some leading to hypotheses of what might occur based on previous experiences, or ideas that have stood up to testing of time. Theories eventually emerge from hypotheses tested over time to the point of "almost objective truth." But nothing can ever be totally "proven." You can only approach it, perhaps with more and more certainty. Philosophies of life, too, arise from thoughts put together in a cohesive, intellectually honest way. They tie things together in examining a particular idea such as , the nature of man, or the origins of the earth. Thoughts are also the master of creativity. The development of the light bulb or wireless transmission all evolved from thoughts by a combination of thinkers–and doers in many instances. But remember: All thoughts of an individual, no matter his genius, evolved partially from thinking by others. And new inventions rely on past inventions for their development.

You Can Rise Above the Level of Thought Within.

You can rise to the higher level of non-thought or observation, and beyond that to pure *mindful energy.*. You can see the various factors that facilitate or prevent changes at the thought level (your programs). The next time you walk from your office to another's, instead of thinking about your mission, become aware of how your feet feel against the floor. Include other senses, listen to the hum of the computers around you, feel the cool air from the vent about you, see the activity all around you. Become an observer rather than a participant in the action and you will find yourself rising above the thought level. In that instant you are safe, secure and at peace.

You are in the moment. You are in the here and now. When you rise above the thought level, your thoughts continue to run through their programming, and you simply observe (listen) to your thoughts as you would a radio program. The thoughts will slow down and dissolve without your trying to shut them out or continue them. Remind yourself that the radio is not you, the air conditioner is not you, and the floor is not you.

Consider another scenario: that of the film we discussed earlier. The movie is not you. When you lose yourself in the story or identify with a character in the movie, turn your attention to knowing that you are observing the movie and to how your mind can shift to becoming the character in the movie. Your thoughts are your internal movie and you can lose yourself in your thoughts–similar to losing your self in a movie. At that point, there is no space between your pure awareness and your thoughts.

Pause here a moment. The next time a thought enters your mind, write it down and read it aloud to yourself. That paper is no more you than the thought you wrote down. Realize the difference. Eventually you will not need to write your thoughts down, but you will "know" exactly what you are thinking, while you are thinking it and be able to separate the thinking process from the purity of your *mindful energy*.

Take any two objects: a fan that is going back and forth and a banner proclaiming "Happy New Year." Without thinking, observe the fan's action. Then observe the banner and its message, again without thinking. After a few tries, you will be able to read the banner and observe yourself reading it. You will also observe the fan without any conscious thoughts interfering with your "being in the moment." When you "observe" your thoughts, they slow down. Therefore, the mind becomes more peaceful and understanding. Too many thoughts tend to clutter the mind. Simplify your thinking for less burnout, less energy expenditure. Each thought can then be reflected upon with great clarity. For example, when a room has too much furniture in it, there is no order or functionality. Choosing where to sit becomes a problem since there are so many options. A cluttered desk impedes progress on a project as all of the objects draw your attention away from focusing on your work.

By simplifying your thinking, you can rise above focus to access your *mindful energy* allowing it to guide you in life. Another way of accomplishing this is to focus on your breathing even when you're not feeling overwhelmed with choices or with life. We will explore breath in the chapter on Passive Meditation, Chapter 6.

This technique is not restricted to objects, but also applies to the thinking that occurs in relationships. When someone calls you on the phone and you feel under attack, or the caller is upset about something which has nothing to do with you, accessing your *mindful energy* will help keep you in the objective, aware field where you can respond without feeling emotionally upset. This process results in a peaceful state of mind. You are then able to observe or listen to your thoughts and evaluate them without being a part of them. You have risen above them to a higher level of *conscious awareness*. Your goal is not to amplify your thoughts, but to eliminate a lot of your brainwork. The resulting clarity of mind allows you to reach that highest part of your being; again, your *mindful energy*.

Observation Without Thought.

Yes, you can observe and not think about it. Do not confuse observation with thinking. Thinking usually supports it, coming in second behind it. Notice how you stop thinking when you first become aware of something. *After a while, you can think and become aware that you are thinking–simultaneously.* When you look at a sunset or listen to words that come from someone else's mouth, you can operate on a purely observation level without thought. At this point, you don't want to amplify thoughts. You can just "be" and, in effect, rise above your thoughts so that you are actually looking down on them and observing their operation. But you have no emotion, only peace of mind, no unfulfilled needs in this level of consciousness, and the essence of your being emerges regardless of the time, situation, or space you are in.

When you get out of your own thoughts to assist people, you have gone from thought to non-thought–just being in the moment where all things are possible. There is no clutter, no distraction, just your pure essence emerging from the muck of past programming into a world of utter calm, peace, and fulfillment in the present. You can then reach out and touch those around you. You are then 'becoming," which is really "being" the best that you can be. Because of your state of mind and actions, you can help those around you. Your mind is now free to function at its highest level, and you can simply observe it–and perhaps wonder at its infinite capabilities at the same time!

Subjective Thought.

Subjective thought is your way of dealing with "the reality out there." You put your own spin on it to "make it yours." This "spin" can be beautiful or ugly, but you have developed it to deal with your life. It is a survival technique you use to exist in today's world. Incorrect perception or interpretation of your thoughts affects your emotional level, and your subsequent actions. It usually occurs if you fail to observe your thoughts objectively because of the filters of your programs. This, in turn, can create stress and imbalance in your body and cause misdirection in the application of your thoughts. But incorrect applications can be modified when you are "aware of being aware" of what is happening, i.e. rise above your thought level. You can perceive points of view holistically, or allow the mind to dig more deeply to explore parts of the whole. You can get a totally different picture of "what is."

Do you want to see only the "tip of the iceberg" of your life, or would you rather access the forces that shape your existence and be able to enjoy evaluation of those around you through enhanced perceptive abilities? The access is through the clearing of your mind and the cleansing of your body to allow you to go beyond your present programs and perceptions.

Your Body's Role

Every thing you have experienced resides within your body. Your future is determined by your being aware of how your body has functioned in the past and in the here and now through the simple process of observation. Within it resides your entire history physically, emotionally, socially, and intellectually. Every feeling, thought or action affects your body, and the more you know about it, the more you will want to protect it from harm and let it fulfill its greatest potential.

Your body responds to 'bad" thoughts in many ways. But your increased heart rate, your increased blood pressure, your increased nervous energy are telling you to slow down, step aside, concentrate on breathing slowly and deeply in and out, and eliminate those forces that created the stress. The effect of stress has become common knowledge with regards to the diseases of mankind.

Mindful energy resides in the body as well as in everything that exists. The body is a physical manifestation of this *mindful energy*. *Mindful energy* is infinite and omnipotent. Consciousness expresses the infinite nature of *mindful energy*.

The Relationship Between Your Brain and Your Body

Your body always changes. It is in a cycle of creation and destruction only to re-create. When the brain and the body are both still, the body can go into homeostasis or perfect balance. This is the optimum state to allow the body to repair itself and to ensure that all your bodily systems are in proper harmony. Health requires the application of brainpower to optimize your physical functioning. You have to think about diet and exercise because your body cannot function properly without them. This leads to better bodily health and the result is optimal use of your potential beyond that of your body. Without good physical health, you cannot function well emotionally, socially, or intellectually. It is the precursor to all that can be attained.

To effectively use your brain's enormous untapped powers, try giving it a silent message: "Only provide me with the thoughts that are of value to me and others mentally and physically." Give it this message at the start of each day. Keep asking the question: Where will this thought lead me? Is this thought of value to me and others?

Your brain functions as a secretary, option provider, friend and sometimes enemy. Your *mindful energy* is capable of directing this sophisticated bio-computer, especially when you actively integrate your *mindful energy* with your "rational mind." Your brain reorganizes itself once you begin to insert new information into its programs. It can release blockages–or can create new ones. It allows the body to heal itself–or can destroy it.

First it must be cleansed before the body can heal itself. The clutter of thousands of thoughts must be cleared so that your *mindful energy* can communicate with your rational mind. There are capabilities inherent in your brain that you can learn to access. The only way you can learn to access these capabilities is to rise above your programmed life and thoughts so that all possibilities can be explored. You must experience observing your thoughts, body, and emotions. Thoughts have a life of their own unless you learn to direct them. You may find ways to heal yourself. You now have the capacity to more fully utilize your brain's almost infinite possibilities to access that greater force that is within you–that of being in complete control of your life–the director of your being.

Your brain is at the center of all your bodily, mental, and emotional action and reactions. It is your choice. The physical brain is the hardware. Your software (programs) resides there. And as in your computer, the software can be changed, refined, discarded, or rebuilt. A desktop computer cannot reorganize its own program. But you can physically insert or modify its software. You can do the same thing with your brain. Recognize and act on the fact that your brain can reorganize itself to comply with your newly expanded programming and/ or software programs. Your brain is more sophisticated than you may think, and reprogramming can take place once you change your physical or mental actions. The essential element is the ability to rise above your thought process and become the "all knowing" presence that is with you at all times.

Relationships Exist Between Thought and Emotion.

An infant chokes. It is frightened (emotion). It then thinks: I cannot breathe. The emotion follows the action but precedes the thought. Later on thoughts can precede emotions and vice versa. But thought is only part of a larger program, which is composed of many thoughts. A program may have a hundred thoughts, which are woven into a complex program. The thought that precedes emotion may be a subconscious thought. Some people may react negatively to criticism and some positively. It is all in the way you have been programmed. All thoughts are subjective. However, you can observe your subjective thoughts from the higher platform of *mindful energy*, which will allow you to remain in a peaceful state of mind, while at the same time evaluating your subjective thoughts. Eventually, your *mindful energy* will replace all your negative or useless thoughts with a program created by peace and harmony.

What About Love, Hate, Anger? Where Do These Fit in "Objective Thought?"

All of the above are simply programs. *Mindful energy* simply views these programs as the subjective reality of the person creating these programs. *Mindful energy* allows that all programs are perfect for your evolvement as a human being providing you realize that these are all programs and not your true self. These are all programs including love.

Love as we presently interpret it is not the same "love" from your higher intelligence. "Love" from your higher intelligence is a knowing that whatever has happened, is happening, and will happen is perfect for the development of your higher self.

Your brain records all your experiences and thoughts and creates programs. Your brain is a sophisticated tool for you to use: it is not your true self. The real you is your *mindful energy* watching the whole show you are creating. All else, such as your body, thoughts, emotions are constantly changing, dissolving, appearing in different forms, all dependent on your subjective programs. Just because you think does not mean that the thought is you.

What Do Thoughts Create in You?

Sadness and all other feelings are created by you by your own thoughts. Your thoughts are your secretary. Your programs (patterns of thought) create all your feeling and emotions. When thoughts appear in your brain, it is a manifestation of past programs interacting with the present events to give you your own particular spin on how you should feel and react to the present events in your life. If you can be objectively aware of your thoughts during this continuous process, then you have the opportunity of discriminating, evaluating and refining your programs to bring out their highest value to you and others.

The Role of Thought in Your Life.

Without thought, we are not human and cannot function in any state of awareness at all. Your function is to identify thoughts both in yourself and others, learn to describe them and evaluate their use. You will then be able to change programming created by thoughts that you have now determined to be irrelevant, outdated, inappropriate, or even harmful. There are many consequences to living in this "thought" modality. Living strictly in the "thought modality" prevents you from contacting different levels of your mind and gaining new knowledge that may not be available to you through your ordinary "thought" channels. Not seeing all the possibilities because of the extreme subjectivity of this element, without utilizing the awareness level to see through it clearly is the bane of man's existence. We all live in the "box" created by our programs. We can optimize our experience by being in the "knowing" state and utilizing it as a platform to see objectively.

ACTIVITY

This is a very useful exercise, which I employed with a friend of mine who happens to be blind from a stroke. Record your thoughts in a tape recorder then play them back. Again, write them down. When Kyle heard his thoughts, he realized that he was not his thoughts. Therefore, he could change them and live a happier life. Playback allowed space between the thoughts and objective awareness.

Why You Should Get Out of this Thought Level (Rational Mind)

I find that the 'knowing" level slows the thoughts coming into my awareness. Redundancy is reduced. Valueless thoughts are reduced. Program change is readily available. There is no active desire to remove unnecessary thoughts; it happens as a result of being in the "knowing" level. The brain exerts its ability to discriminate because it is not busy with its usual flood of thinking, most of which is not necessary. The brain then reorganizes itself to create new value programs for you.

How You Can Get Out of, or Beyond this Thought Level?

Here is an example:

Imagine yourself being in a room. It is clearly defined by its space, layout, light, windows, and entry and exit locations. You can "choose" to stay in this constant environment by doing what you always do when there. You do things the same way, you think the same way, and you move your body in the same way as you have done thousands of times before. Your programs have put you there, and you have chosen unconsciously–and somewhat less consciously!–to accept the situation as your own reality. Your future and your present are dictated to you by your perceptions and actions and reactions of the past, and you become robotic as you face things the same way you have done for years. Your life is being directed by forces that you have taken unto you, and you may have lost control of everything around you and within you.

When your brain pops a thought into consciousness in answer to a situation, don't take it for granted that it is the "correct thought." Ask yourself the question: What other options are available to me? Then choose the option you feel addresses the situation the best and also benefits all the people involved. It may not even be the right question or situation your brain is responding to. It may well have misread the information. You are able to get out of your "thought room" by the act of simply observing your immediate surroundings or being aware of your physical movements, in conjunction with listening to your thoughts in your "aware" zone.

- First, realize that you are in this room of your own making by your own past and present physical, emotional, social and intellectual experiences, both from within yourself and coming from all those people, places, and things around you.
- Accept yourself as an eternal learner. Learn to become an observer. Do not try to control, force, or dismiss your thoughts.
- Retrain your mind to ask: "Why am I using this program and is it of value to me and all others involved?"
- Record your thoughts and either read them back out loud or listen on your tape recorder.
- Ask: "Where will this take me?"
- Ask: "What will be the cause and effect if I follow this thought

and place it into action?"

- Ask: "What are the other options available to me in this situation?"
- Play-act the different options and the ensuing cause and effect results.

For example, the following diagram presents just one hypothetical thought a person might be having, its description, and the level of functioning as the person has this thought. It probes some facilitators and blockers of clear thinking, and possible positive and negative results that could emanate from just this one thought. This process enables you to become master of your thoughts. You can discard the inappropriate, unkind, and valueless from your being and replace them with selfless thoughts that lead to kind and loving actions.

Thought	Reasons For Its Existence	Blockers of Looking at Throught More Objectively	Facilitators of Looking at Throught More Objectively	Possible Positive Results and Change	Possible Negative Results and Change
Give this a try. List one thought below and fill in the blanks			Asking questions; meditation Seeking further options	Conscious thought; *Mindful Energy*	
Jonh does not accurately call the tennis shots when close to the lines.	When playing tennis, John consistently called the shots out when they were in.	John won the game unfairly.	Wht is the reason John is acting in this manner?	John may have an eyesight problem, which prevents him from seeing clearly	(A) Tell John (B) Say nothing. Cause and effect of each option

Should There be Differences between Thought and Consciousness?

Yes, because you are then able to view your thinking from the platform of pure consciousness, which enables you to direct your thoughts and refine them in order to evolve your self as a human being.

What Effects Can There be by Not Separating Thought from Consciousness?

Semi-conscious states of mind which include being directed by your programming, which may be harmful and inappropriate to the current situation, events, and relationships in your life.

What Effects Can There be by Separating Thought from Consciousness?

The ability to discriminate and direct your thinking; cultivating a conscious state of mind wherein you can live your life in peace and harmony with every event, situation, and person you come into contact with. By becoming more creative, productive, efficient, healthy (physically and mentally).

ACTIVITY

Now try writing down one of your own thoughts and work your way through the process as we just shown you.

How Can Changing My Level of Thought Change My Perceptions of Reality, Situations, Feelings, or Thoughts?

When you allow space between your thoughts and your "knowing" level, you can begin to see and feel the differences between playing out different options to each situation.

- Your perceptions change with each option.
- Your feelings change with each option.
- Your thoughts change because you are introducing new elements with each option.
- Your emotions change as your thoughts change.

Now work through the following diagram to see how it relates to your emotions, actions, and behavior.

Emotions	Perceptions of Precursors to its Existence	Blockers of Looking at Emotion More Objectively	Facilitators of Looking at Emotion More Objectively	Possible Positive Results and Change	Possible Negative Results and Change
Anger	Someone is not acting ethically	Failure to observe your thoughts and seeking options	Asking Questions; meditation; seeking further options	Conscious thought; *Mindful Energy*	Acting on your emotion without using prior "knowing" level and causing additional stress

Now try it with an action or behavior.

Action or Behavior	Perceptions of Precursors to its Existence	Blockers of Looking at Emotion More Objectively	Facilitators of Looking at Emotion More Objectively	Possible Positive Results and Change	Possible Negative Results and Change

How Can You Access the Highest Level of Awareness and Understanding in One Specific Area of Your Life?

Through observation. See how you can reach that clear space within your mind.

Relationships Exist Between Thought And Awareness.

Knowing = Awareness = *mindful energy* = space

- No space (awareness) between your pure automatic reactions and your thoughts.
- There is space between pure awareness of being aware (knowingness) and your thoughts.

SUMMARY: UNDERSTANDING THOUGHTS AND THINKING

- Thoughts are "thinking" you.
- You can learn to be director of your thoughts and choose to act.
- Thought is the steering wheel of your mind.
- You can learn to observe your thoughts.
- You can rise to the higher level of non-thought or observation.
- You realize that thoughts are not you.
- You can learn to redefine your thoughts to benefit you and others.
- Your creativity is enhanced when you direct your thoughts from this higher level of observation.

- Your physical well being is enhanced when stress is eliminated as a result of your being in the observational mode.
- Negative emotions will dissolve as a result of your being in the observation mode.

5

PROGRAMS AND PROGRAMMING

What You Will Learn:

Problems or Perception?

We have no problems. We perceive a situation as a problem because of our subjective programming that interprets certain situations as problems. In reality everything just "is". We create our own subjective interpretation of "what is". You get angry at insignificant events. You get sad when someone criticizes you. You appear conscious. You are using all of your five senses. You walk, talk, eat, drink, etc. Your perceptions are created from this "conscious" viewpoint. But how conscious are we really if we react to every possible stimulus out there?

Recognize the situation. Define it. Describe it. Determine at what level this situation is affecting you and those around you. Determine its history or etiology. Determine how important this situation is to you. Determine alternatives to current and past behavior, actions and reactions to the identified situation. Look at the situation in terms of programming, observing it, conscious awareness of its existence and affects on you and those around you. Meditate to reach your inner essence, that level of thought- non-thought, then rise to the level of observation of yourself, separating the situation from your *mindful energy*. Be in the present. "Know" the "gap" that permits you to rise above the problem. Interpretation of the situation takes place at many different levels, and at different times, and in different places, and with or without different people.

Programmed Part of the Self	Re: Actions	Consequences
Higher Self Mindful Energy	Observing	Self Realization

Everyone wants to be "happy". Have you ever considered the benefits of being "peaceful", neither happy nor unhappy? The razor's edge. Perfect balance between extremes. This is the perfect place to view all the reflections that the mind creates. Be amused, interested, entertained, etc. by all that goes on around you; all within the envelope of "peacefulness and wholeness"- (i.e. holiness).

The life force that courses through the body can be expanded into a larger flow which could regenerate your cells throughout your body. The "switch" is there–you need to locate it and learn how to use it in order to draw on the infinite powers of this universal field where everything is possible.

Once you can get out of the box you can opt to start utilizing the unlimited energy, unlimited creativity, unlimited peacefulness, unlimited power, unlimited security, that is there for you to use. You **can** influence world peace.

Healing can be instantaneous, physical endurance extended, creativity enhanced, peacefulness extended to all aspects of your life.

You now have the ability and skills to become pro-active on drawing from the infinite will of your being; power, security, ecstasy, and sheer joy of, in being a part of the universal field of life.

How Do You Experience Life?

You are experiencing life from the narrow perspective of your own personal programs. You can let them operate you, or you can learn to direct them at a highly conscious, aware level. You can live within a framework or a box of your own creation, or get out of the "box" and live in harmony with all that is. You can explore this framework (programming) to find a door to the next room and reach higher purposes in life. You can live your life consciously, in a higher state of awareness, until you reach that state of *mindful energy* that you can apply to all aspects of your life at all times. You can learn to place your life into global, universal fields that will enhance and broaden your life as you go beyond your individual mode. You will utilize your innate *mindful energy* to direct your thoughts. You will evolve from the tail wagging the dog, to wagging your own tail.

The accumulated residual effects of our experiences resulted in patterns of behavior called programs. These programs now dictate our behavior, actions, and reactions to everyone and everything in our environment. Unless something changes the thoughts, behaviors and feelings within us, they will continue to dictate the ways we respond to our own lives and to the lives of others.

People of all ages can rise to their greatest potential: to live life fully, in the present, unhampered by past programs that may be determining their feelings, beliefs, attitudes, actions or behavior. Through the use of basic understandings, this information provides roads to life's greatest fulfillment. These basic understandings enhance the intellectual, physical, social and emotional qualities of life. They serve as guideposts and the basis of lessons and activities that will develop a more complete understanding, and enable the achievement of the purposes of the program.

Today you rush to get things done. Something happens and you are happy. Another event occurs and you are sad. You don't realize that you are an actor on a stage, being directed by programs you were unaware of–including those you put there yourself. But are you on automatic pilot? Has someone else programmed your responses, your thoughts, and your emotions? Are you a robot?

Everything that happens is subject to internal programs that reside in your brain. Therefore, if you are a pre-programmed being and this programming was put into your "software" when you were brought up by parents, peers, and teachers, was this programming appropriate, sufficient, and fulfilling? Can it now work as a beacon guiding you toward your highest essence of being, or is it in fact, deterring your from becoming all that you wish to be, feel, and desire? You may harbor deep-seated anger, distrust, or even hatred for your parents or others from your past. They imposed their programs on you when you were vulnerable, young, not strong enough to rebel, and inexperienced. But they, too, were programmed by their own parents. They did not know that there were other, more acceptable ways of doing things. Now that you realize what happened, you have the opportunity to correct your own inappropriate programs. You can also let go, accept what happened, and move on.

Think about this analogy: If your mathematical computer program said that 2+2=5, you would certainly correct it. Otherwise, all of your future calculations and decisions based upon these present calculations would be incorrect. Do you want a computer program telling you what to do? If you do not correct your inappropriate programs you can be assured that the experiences of your life will not improve. They will most likely deteriorate. But you must understand how they came to be imprinted on your brain and may be dictating to you as you read.

Our brains operate essentially like computers; that is why we were able to create computers. They are a simplified reflection of how we work.

As we learn to identify, describe and explore our present programming we can begin to evaluate the impact of past programming on our lives today. As individuals examine their present behaviors, beliefs and emotions objectively, they will begin to appreciate their negative and positive effects. They can keep those aspects that enhance their lives, and discard those which hamper their development. In the process they will recognize their own power to change themselves and others in enlightened, exhilarating ways.

You are asleep now functioning robotically from your programmed level; you want to be awake functioning from your *mindful energy* level.

You are your thoughts—the living result of an accumulation of experiences that have become intricately woven into the person you are now. Memories of events that happened many years ago may have resulted in scenarios which are affecting your life today. You may be operating inadequately today because the programs of the past are not appropriate for today's situations—you have changed, society has changed, situations constantly change. *Worst of all, you may not even be aware of their operating within you at this very moment.*

Fixed programs create conflicts. Flexible programs allow you to harmonize with what "is". Your behavior may have been appropriate at the time, and emotions that may have risen in both your conscious and unconscious self due to your programming, are now leading your life physically, emotionally, socially, and intellectually wherever you go and whatever you do. Some of these past programs and resulting present feelings, actions, and thoughts are wasteful and unproductive. If the conscious ability to change does not take place within you, this scenario will remain a part of you, and you will not be able to attain the highest levels of self-fulfillment that you are capable of and desire.

Like ripples in the pond, as we begin this work individually, our influence will spread to others and eventually benefit everyone in the world today.

Expectations

"Expectations" set you up to create unhappiness. You create a model in your mind as to how events should turn out, and when the actual event does not match up to the model you created in your mind, conflict and unhappiness are created.

A simple solution to your unhappiness from unmet expectations is to step outside your "box" and observe the expectation from that still, quiet place in your mind. There's no need to ask if the expectation is reasonable or unreasonable. In fact, it just "is". Once we realize it's not important how we view it, we will be able to release it and simply allow whatever "is" to be. Expectations are an excellent example of a program which we learned and we taught ourselves, and which has no possibility of serving us.

What Is a Program?

Programs are the filters in your mind through which all objective reality pass through prior to becoming "your" experience. A program is a set of thoughts, feelings, emotions and/or actions that operates within you and affect many aspects of your life today. Your caretakers began your programming at birth. As your social world expanded, so did your programming. As you matured, you developed your own programs in response to stimuli in your environment. Where you are today is a combination of all three program sources: genetics, programming by others, and your own programming.

Specifically, events as a sudden traumatic experience, receiving an award for an essay, a domineering father, and intensely jealous sibling, being in a bad neighborhood or school, getting involved an after school activity program, or perhaps being mentored by an extraordinary person all activated responses in you. Those responses shaped your behavior for the next time the stimulus occurred. As long as you are awake, you can not escape these influences and the ways each one affected one or more of your programs.

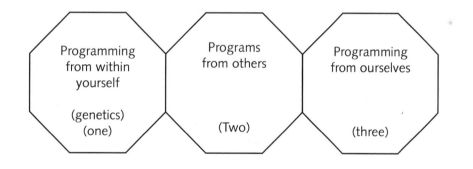

PROGRAM EXAMINATION

You have nothing to fear by examining your programming. As long as you are unaware of the conscious and unconscious forces operating within you, you will be unable to move forward in a harmonious and peaceful manner. If you are not conscious of their operation, you can do nothing to change their influence. You will not have the "free will" to rise above your programmed mind until you proactively make an effort to do so.

The first step is to realize that you are programmed. The second step is to observe your programs–this can be done by simply writing down the thoughts that are going through your mind. The third step is to meditate on an active (dual tracking) level (more on this later) so that you can go through the door and divest yourself of this programmed box you live in. You will not live fully until you accomplish this action.

When you learn to identify the signals (physical feelings, thoughts, and emotions) of these hidden forces you will understand how they operate. Only then can you forge a relationship between your material subjective world and the unseen world; using your *mindful energy* to guide you through the process. This will create a new, more evolved world.

Your life continues to be programmed every second. You can continue to reinforce programs that create unhappiness or develop a new program that creates peacefulness.

Does Programming Create Your Experiences or Do Your Experiences Result in Their Creating Your Programming–or Can They Be Interactive?

From birth–perhaps even before–your mind, emotions, and body have been bombarded by billions of bits of data. You ignored some, took parts from others, or perhaps even took an entire experience into yourself. During this process you may have put more weight on some information. You wound up interpreting it both subjectively and objectively. You were programmed to respond positively to some information and negatively to others. You also programmed yourself at the same time. Sound confusing? Let's look at a simple situation: Joe always eats scrambled eggs for breakfast. He expects to enjoy them. Joe has a series of experiences that became routine–a defined series of behaviors, expectations, feelings and thoughts called a program. This program then defined the experiences he would have every time he sat down at the breakfast table. But he lacked the joy of a brand new experience every morning; his programmed self was on automatic.

One day he bit into an eggshell and it lodged in his throat. It sent chills through out his body. He tried to spit the eggshell out of his mouth with no success. The more he thought about it, the more he wanted to rid himself of the shell. He felt nauseous; it was making him sick, so he never ate eggs again. A new program dictated that he avoids eggs entirely. But in the process it destroyed the various pleasurable parts of his previously established set of behaviors, feelings and expectations. He was unable to separate the bad part that destroyed his enjoyable experience from the satisfaction he used to derive from his scrambled egg breakfast.

Programs are created both internally and externally, although their evolution, operation, and results may be intertwined. As demonstrated in the previous diagram, we are a composite of three programs: internally (genetic), imposed by others, and created by ourselves. Explore what "internally" means to you. Was this intuitive or because someone else said it; or did you read about it? In Joe's case his over reaction to an eggshell may have originated by observing someone else's over reaction, or from something he read about salmonella on unwashed eggs, or when he was a child and he became ill after biting into an eggshell.

How Does Change Take Place?

Joe did not take the time or effort to probe deeply into his current abhorrence of eggs. Therefore, he could not take control of the situation and salvage what was left. He simply and simplistically–avoided the experience. This by the way, became a new, inappropriate program that deprived him of the opportunity to experience the tastes he enjoyed in the past. Had he been aware of his inappropriate programming based on one incident, he could have explored the experience rationally. He could have figured out what he could do the next time he was offered scrambled eggs. Joe could have followed the steps below to better assess his problem.

- Commit to writing what he is thinking, feeling and doing at all times. (He is thinking that he does not want to feel that way at breakfast again.)
- Know why he is doing the things that he does, thinking the things that he thinks and feeling the way he does (He is rejecting all scrambled eggs because he is afraid of the threat of another eggshell). Was his response objective, rational, logical, or appropriate?
- Evaluate their positive and negative impacts on his life (He cannot enjoy eggs now, he is retaining the fear of eggshells, and this inappropriate program takes effort) and develop options that will delete the negative aspects and retain the positive aspects.
- Make the determination that now is the time to begin his personal process of renewal growth. (He will chew more carefully, savoring each mouth full of delicious eggs and by doing so he will be aware of any eggshell in his food. He will unburden himself from past, inappropriate thoughts, feelings and actions, leaving him more time and energy to spend on present objectively examined situations).
- Carry through this process of change to all of his life's experiences (and in this process he may even be able to change the lives around him. We hope so!)

The result? He will explore issues that he developed himself, those imposed upon him by others, and those that operate from within that he will learn to identify. He will use his feelings, actions, and thoughts to better analyze what happened. He will better understand why they occurred and be able to make better choices. He will function better by developing more appropriate programs to enjoy life to the fullest.

ACTIVITY

To understand any present situation and your reactions to it, you need to evaluate it from the perspective of your existing programs and the perspective of all the options available to you. Follow the steps given below to face any situation and evaluate its effect on you and others!

- Describe in writing the present situation and its effects on your present feelings, thoughts and behavior, physical reactions, energy level.
- Ask yourself "Is this thought of value to me and others? Determine whether or not your reactions, thought processes and behaviors are appropriate and objective, logical and rational. Make certain that you have examined all facets of the situation.
- Fast forward to the effects your thoughts and behavior will have in the future.
- List all the possible options you could utilize in this situation. And how each option would create a different effect on you and others.
- Decide on which option will best create harmony, peace and understanding between you and all the people involved in the particular situation.

- Recognize that your past programming may or may not now be appropriate in the present situation. Say to yourself: I understand what preceded this event. I will not act or react as I did in the past. I will not hold on to outmoded behavior, feelings and thoughts. I will now examine, as objectively as possible, present events unimpeded by prior judgments. I will act and react based on evaluation of "what is," rather than "what was."

Write down ten of your thoughts, feelings, and/or behaviors during the course of the day that involved responses to various situations. Write your stream of thoughts or feelings just as they are thought or felt. Do not interpret, analyze or change them. Then look at them after work or school and read out loud what you wrote as if you were reading someone else's writing. Now enter some of them to the chart below. Put the event in the 1st column, your thought, feeling or behavior in the 2nd column. In the 3rd column determine if the thought, feeling or behavior is of value to you. In the 4th column determine for yourself whether or not your response was objective, rational, logical and appropriate. Be objective and honest at all times. In the 5th column list the possible options that could have been available to you in each of these situations. Let us do five for you that present very different levels of functioning to get you started.

Event	Thought, Feeling, Behaviour	Is this thought, feeling, or behavior of value to me and others around me? Answer yes or no and why	Was response objective, rational, logical, appropriate?	New Program Possible Options
Lunch bells rings	I am not hungry but I don't want to be left alone; rejection, fear, insecurity		Yes _____ No _____	
The driver ahead of me is driving erratically	Angry, irritated, annoyed		Yes _____ No _____	
My boss criticized me for being slow in completing a job	Hatred		Yes _____ No _____	
I sidestepped a little puddle	Irritation, annoyance, fear of rejection		Yes _____ No _____	
I stepped into a small puddle	Asserting my independence		Yes _____ No _____	

New Programs

The first example may appear to be rather simplistic. But let's take another look. What if you had just had a snack? The lunch bell rings and everyone starts to leave the office. Are you really hungry? Do your actually "feel" hunger pangs at the sound of the bell–just like one of Pavlov's dogs? Or do you just want to leave your desk, and join the crowd? Your subsequent behavior–and your feelings about that behavior may or may not be what you want. Do you follow the crowd, or do you do what you really want to do? You have to be alert to what programs are driving your actions, and remember to review what other options are available.

The second example seems straightforward enough. But is it? Is it possible that your serious accident just last week affected your response to an infinitesimally small change in the direction of the car ahead of you? Might you have fallen asleep momentarily or not been fully attentive to your driving and not seen why the driver was driving that way? Your response might be the same response your father used when he drove behind an erratic driver. Your anger might compel you to gun the accelerator and pass him--- leading to an accident. Once you examine your anger, consider the possible source of it, realize your anger is not you, and then you can observe your choices and access your *mindful energy* to make the right one. If the erratic driver is not risking your life, what difference does his driving make to you?

Your response could be rational or irrational. You could feel strongly about what happened–(one program) even if it was not appropriate–or you could have brushed it off (another program). The choice is yours as long as you are aware of all the circumstances surrounding the incident. Furthermore, would you do the same thing differently if it happened again–and again–and again? Would it start to "get under your skin?" Perhaps you are beginning to get the idea.

Consider the third situation very carefully. Where did your feelings of hatred come from (a program in the past)? Should you even have thoughts like this? Were you aware of your boss' own problem that caused him to act the way he did? And why are your feelings so strong? Perhaps you feel that a job well done is more important than completing it quickly. Could you have evaluated the situation, understood his problem, and sidetracked his apparently difficult behavior? Your own words and actions both in the immediate situation and at the precise moment of the incident can be changed. Maybe your best action is to walk away–even from the job itself.

The fourth and fifth situations are similar enough at first glance. A puddle existed, but you have behaved differently because of your feelings from the past. And why did you behave the way you did? Similar programming, someone yelling at you for splashing when you were a child, can cause totally dissimilar behaviors and feelings today. Then, you were humiliated and shamed, so you sought to avoid those feelings in the future. Today, you are not concerned about a caretaker's disapproval so you are free to enjoy the sensation of splashing in the rain. Same circumstances, a different evaluation.

We showed five scenarios that might have resulted in certain thoughts and feelings. But they had no basis in reality unless you chose to attribute reality to them consciously or unconsciously. Thus, we can say that all thoughts and feelings are subjective. When you force them to rise to a conscious level you can begin to act on them. Not before! How can you change if you do not know what is really happening?

You have begun to look at "good" or effective and "bad" or ineffective programs you have. Now let's look at one of your "good" programs and see how it can affect you.

At first you can obtain a better objective viewpoint by writing the event and the above steps. Thereafter you will be able to do these steps within your mind as the event unfolds.

Below is a box with arrows extending from it. Give your "good" program a title and write it in the center of the box. On the arrows write your perceptions of good affects the "good" program has on you.

But there are many examples of "bad" programs out there as well. Can you think of a program you feel is working badly for you?

Below is a box with arrows extending from it. Write the title of your "bad" program in the center of the box. On the arrows write your perceptions of effects the "bad" program has on you.

The first order of business was to realize what you were thinking, feeling or doing. You were operating in fields that appeared to be appropriate (your "good" program) or inappropriate (your "bad" program) in your present situation. You may have been functioning (albeit poorly) in these narrow "fields". Were your behaviors (programs) placed there by parents, teachers, society, media and your friends? It doesn't matter. When you observe your present program objectively you can then begin to enlarge your field of awareness. You can explore the effects these programs had on your experience of life and their affects on the experiences of everyone around you. When you explored the good and bad programs were you aware of the relative impact others had in developing them? Did your bad program have more input from others? Did your good program have less? I have found that good programs have more input from within your *mindful energy*. However, where did your input arise? Was it, in fact at least partially influenced by forces outside yourself?

You Need Programmed Behavior

There are many simple programs from your past that are operating within you at this very moment. If you had to think about every aspect of your daily shaving or bathing routine, your mind would not be free to explore your world. And if you had to consciously locate the turn signal whenever you made a turn while driving, the effort involved could well result in you hitting a pedestrian. When you are approaching the checkout lane and another shopper is slightly ahead of you, you automatically defer to him. There is no need to think about it, unless your previous hang-ups (programs) tell you to beat him there. Programs help with simple behaviors. But many programs from your past and those that you use today are far more complicated. What happens when two programs conflict with each other? You may have a "loving program" that says your actions will be loving because you have programmed yourself or someone else programmed you to be that way. But you may resent this "loving program" when someone has hurt you or your family in some way. You feel compromised.

Furthermore, you may think that you are directing your own script but unconscious needs may be directing your present actions. You think you are conscious because you use your five senses. But you may be on "automatic" much of the time. You are the actor, but the script may have been written by your past programming.

Can you change your outlook on life if your body and personality type have been programmed into you genetically? Suppose you are a 6 foot tall woman with a heavy boned frame, and yet you desire to become a movie starlet, or you've always wanted to be a jet pilot, but your eyesight is too poor to qualify; your genetic programming prevents you from achieving those goals based on what others tell you are the qualifications for each ambition. You can accept the disappointment of your programming, or acknowledging the difficulty in achieving those goals, you can either change them or do what it takes by changing your personal programming. The pilot explores the possibility of laser eye surgery, and the ingénue diets herself into thinness. My position is that, given knowledge of yourself genetically and environmentally (experientially), you can be in charge of the way you view your life. It is the awareness of the genetic influences which will allow you to change them if they no longer serve you. Again, objective observation is the key. Wake up to them, observe them and then take charge to either retain or reject them.

Our Comfort Level Affects Stability and Change of Behavior.

Imagine yourself in a room watching television. You feel comfortable and relaxed. Is this a manifestation of boredom, repetitive action and reaction? How long will this go on? How can you have a desire to get out of a comfortable room when you do not realize that other rooms exist? What excitement are you passing up by staying in the room? You have to examine your behavior and your feelings before you can really accept yourself as being comfortable. Only then can you evaluate its restraints or possibilities. Are you truly as aware of what you are feeling and doing as you can be at every given moment?

Much of what you do and say is automatic. You take a drink of water when you are thirsty. The action is automatic. You put your foot on the brake pedal to get into gear as you start your car. The action is automatic. These scenarios can carry over into more important aspects of your life. You do not think of the consequences of your feelings or actions, and even they become automatic. They are programmed, you are hardly aware of their existence, and, Yes! They are comfortable! On the other hand, change can take place when you realize that your comfort level may not be getting you anywhere. Your taking the time to read this book indicates that you are not comfortable with the way you feel, think, act, and react to conditions in your life.

Conversely, you may have bad feelings as you live your daily life. Why do you continue thinking the same thoughts, feeling the way you do, and behaving the way you to despite your negative feelings? They are uncomfortable, but they, too, can create the impetus for changing your behavior, feelings, and thoughts. Try this to begin understanding the effects of uncomfortable situations in your life.

For example: you begin to be aware that you shy away from greeting strangers, you find yourself giving up too easily on any number of seemingly simple tasks, or you would rather stay home than call to get tickets to a show. These behaviors may appear to be totally different at first glance, but look again. Does a parallel thread run through them?

Could previous programming have led you to shyness, risk avoidance, and "laziness"? Is it possible that your parents created these behaviors through patterns of verbal suggestions that said explicitly or were implied that "you can't do this."? "I don't think that you are capable of doing anything"? You may have subsequently inferred from these remarks and so many others like them that because you were incapable of many things you generalized and established programs that said, "I am not good with strangers." "I might as well not even try to accomplish anything," or "I won't enjoy or learn anything anyway so why try?" The objective is not to actively explore the past, but to observe and allow thoughts to come into our conscious awareness and in turn observe those thoughts. And then ask yourself the prime question: Is this thought of value to me and all others concerned?

Results of Freedom From Inappropriate Programming.

Now is the time to evaluate your existing programs and how they are operating in the present time. When you know through observation (not digging into the past), where you are now, and where you can go physically, emotionally, socially and intellectually you can allow your mind and body to climb out of their self imposed jails of programmed thoughts, actions and feelings. You will become much more alert and aware of some of the consequences in your life of programming by yourself and others. Perhaps you are now beginning to recognize that some programmed feelings, thoughts, and actions can result in trapped behavior, lack of free will, and the feeling of being a prisoner in a world not of your own making. *When you learn to change the process, the product will change.*

Each time this happens you rise to a higher plain–a higher form of functioning and enjoyment as you unravel the threads of your life. It is ongoing and continuous as you actively involve yourself wholeheartedly in examining your existence and attain the highest level of functioning that you can. You will be free to determine how you will live the rest of your life; climb high on its wings and soar to the greatest heights of which you are capable. Your mind, being freed of its tremendous weight, can now find joy and true love–for so many people, places, and things around you. And in the process you will find that your new persona attracts those around you as they welcome the changes in you and enjoy you for who you truly are–not the person you were programmed to be.

As you read we hope that you are beginning to look at your present actions, feelings and thoughts and their results in your life today. Now you can determine whether or not you want to keep these thoughts, feelings, and behaviors or let them go, enabling you to rise to a higher level of consciousness where you are the master, rather than being the slave of your programming.

What Lies Beyond Understanding Programs?

Experiences, the objective observation of yourself and others, and investigation of the thought processes involved will eventually lead to your fuller awareness of what is going on through a process of dual tracking. We will examine each in turn: experiencing, objectivity, observation, thought, consciousness and awareness, and dual tracking. The ultimate goal is "Self" Realization. The realization that your true "Self" is not your personality or your thoughts or your body. Your true self is your pure core of *"mindful energy"*, which if you access it can guide you consciously in each moment of the present so that each moment is self- fulfilling in itself.

Your Programmed Self:

The accumulated residual effects have resulted in patterns of behavior, called *programs* that now dictate your behavior, actions, and reactions to everyone and everything around you. Unless you change the thoughts, behaviors, and feelings within you they will continue into the future and dictate the ways you respond to your own life and to the lives of those around you for the rest of your life. Learning how to simply observe all of your present programs will enable you to change in positive ways. The act of observing allows your thoughts to slow down; the mind becomes more peaceful and understanding; less energy is utilized; less brain burnout that occurs when too much data is inputted. But your future is really the present–the today of your life as you can become more than you are. As you read this book you will look at programs. You will observe them, identify them and describe them. As you observe them you will focus on evaluating their present value in your life. We will then show you how to become more aware, more objective, and more conscious of not only your life and its behaviors, but also those of people around you. You will then be able to evaluate their impact on your life–and yours on theirs! You will learn how to select and deselect programs to suit your enhanced, knowledgeable self, and in the process learn to modify your life through specific techniques to guide you to a higher level of awareness–this is called your *mindful energy*, your inner essence, or your higher being. As you focus, your future will become brighter as you realize that your life today holds excitement and pleasures you did not even know about. John Dewey back in 1903 perhaps said it best: "by doing you become". That is, by observing your present programs you can become–all that you want to be! We are here to discover that our true self is non-material, but a *mindful energy* around which our material bodies have been built.

Why Are You Here?

I believe we are all here to evolve into the highest form of human we are capable of being. This book will examine the possibility of enriching your life to its fullest level of growth while you are here. Otherwise, what purpose does your presence here on earth have?

How Did Your Life Begin?

You entered life as a clean plate with nothing on it–with no good– no bad. At first you had sensations–sensations of pain, pleasure, roundness (from your mother's nipple, her finger, or the round cap of your bottle) and other concepts (yes, you could not speak them, write them, or fully understand them, but they existed!). From your very first days on earth you had physical, emotional, even social and intellectual encounters. You began to have perceptions of love or rejection, expectation and denial. And certain patterns emerged that accompanied you for many years as you went through childhood, puberty, and eventual adulthood. These patterns wove themselves into intricate behavioral, feeling, observing, valuing, and evaluating programs, all of which impinged on you physically, emotionally, socially and intellectually. So your programming began, and you are now the embodiment of your entire past. For example, memories of a bad relationship with your mother may be clouding your present perceptions of your life and of those around you. You may misinterpret behaviors of your best friend because certain programs from the past make you unable to have an objective view of his actions today. You may feel that, based on your mother's ill-conceived expectations of you, your friend now perceives you, in effect, through the eyes of your mother. And you may still be allowing your life to be programmed by others. You may have allowed outside events and people to create your experience of life because you have lost conscious control of your programs and experiences. You may have become robotic in your thinking and emoting.

What Are Your Options Now?

You now have the opportunity to enjoy the many facets of your life and function more profitably by a process of defining your own life and its actions. When everyone was thinking and acting the same way, you may have behaved the same way because you did not see alternatives. No one pointed out different ways you could live your life–thinking, feeling, and acting differently from those around you. You were not aware that you could do things in your own way, at your own time, and in a place of your choosing. Your "being" was simply imposed on you from external forces. When you learn to become a true creator of your own experience, you and everyone you come into contact with will benefit. Then you are on your way to true freedom. You are no longer trapped in the box created by programs that were entered into your brain prior to your realizing their impact and their cause/effect relationship. The change and freedom in your life and your ability to choose your experience will ripple outward. The old programs that had directed your life may have continued through generations. The option to choose your experience will provide the opportunity for other people, especially your children, to change their programs. Having the choice will enhance everyone's life.

Learn To Explore the Present/Live in the Present

By exploring the present you do not have to repeat your past programming which may have been acceptable at that time but is inappropriate now. You need the skills to explore its effect on your life today. That's what you are going to learn. To live in the present is not to deliberately delete all of your past programs. If your brain brings a thought to the forefront of your mind, you have to look at it objectively and ask: Is this thought, feeling or behavior of value to me and everyone around me. What effect is it having on me today? You will learn to pick those that are of value to you. By being in a highly aware intelligent state of mind without any analyzing or thinking you will simply "know". You chose certain thoughts over others in your past. You were programmed to do so. However, the beginning is to simply observe these thoughts, feelings and actions while you are in a knowing or aware state of mind. You are automatically rising to a higher state of mind when you are aware of observing your thoughts. You will learn about what thoughts you can now eliminate or diminish–and enjoy extra time by not dwelling on them–you will be better able to live your present life fully without all that excess baggage.

Your experiences of the past may not have been good or may have been good at that time but now you will be able to look at and absorb them in a positive way. Another way of saying is that people's behaviors are not directed to you personally, but are reflections of their own programs. Therefore, you do not have to be affected negatively by them. You do not have to let past programming of yourself and others influence your life today. You can learn from your past history–and have compassion for those who may have acted unwisely. On a universal level you can change the way you use your mind. You can rise to this level of higher intelligence and eventually you will be peaceful within yourself and with the rest of the world. Harmony, love and peace will prevail. Helping others will become your prime purpose.

Explore the present. (NOTE: Thoughts are usually about the past or the future. Not the here and now.) How is a particular program working today? No need to explore the past. Focus on the present. The only question is whether your program promotes peace and harmony within yourself and with all concerned. When you observe a program be aware and write down what comes up in your mind. Do not "actively" pursue any thoughts. These are just some of the important ideas you have to consider when going down the paths to change.

What Should You Think About as You Read?

Now is the opportune moment to ask yourself how this experience of life happens. Look around you. People are constantly in a whirl. They must always be busy. They feel lost if they are not doing something, no matter how trivial it may appear to an outsider. They never stop to reflect and wonder how and why they are experiencing. They are not aware of what forces are now functioning to make them the way they are, or what or who is creating this experience called "life in the present". In essence, they are not aware of how their programs are guiding their every step. Society, too, is built on a foundation of beliefs, desires, expectations, and models of how things should be done. You might call them universal programs because many people function based on programming that the culture or society endorses. When reality does not match up with these models, desires and expectations, negative emotions appear en masse and manifest themselves in irrational thought and behavior. You experience a sense of conflict, sadness and unhappiness.

You may be programming your ongoing behavior repetitively today based on previous programs that have come either from your own experience or adopting societies programs, your friends programs, your parents programs, etc.

These past behaviors can result in a truly vicious cycle of responding with patterns of behavior that are not viable today. These patterns prevent your objective intelligence from examining each scenario from all angles. You may also be programming those you meet based on your past expectations, experiences, or beliefs so that now you expect certain feelings, behaviors, and thoughts from that individual regardless of today's totally different stage. Do you operate this way?

Now is the time to explore the actuality of your life and its potential to expand your vision to evolve and develop into the best person that you can be. You can learn to change your programs that have been created in the past so that your vision of yourself and those around you becomes your life today and tomorrow.

Consider this: There is no past or future. Only the eternal "now" moment exists. Your mindset determines how you look at your world. Right now you may realize that much of your experience of life resides in the past or future–very infrequently in the "present". You have been programmed to function in this manner. All that is necessary is to know what you are telling yourself in the here and now and determine what state you are now in. But remember, all this takes place in your "present". Throughout your reading we provide you with ideas to activate your mind. Refer to them often as guideposts. These ideas will be presented in depth as you proceed. They will serve as pathways to higher levels of functioning within you on a daily basis. They will help you to reach your objectives—inner peace within your highest intellectual essence at all times.

The Possibility of Choice

There are no "negative" or "bad" situations. "Value" judgments are also programs. It is up to me to choose to interpret any event or situation in the optimum manner in order to serve myself and others.

If a person is running off a program that is inappropriate, then I would allow it to run its course while being in a loving, unconditionally accepting frame of mind. After the "run off" there may be an opportunity to present options to this person to benefit him/her.

If you cannot stay in the same material space because of fear of physical abuse then leave and write that person a loving, understanding letter and propose options to continue the relationship for his consideration.

Just how I choose to perceive another person's and my own feelings, actions, and thoughts affect my consciousness of the experience. It becomes objective and non-judgmental as I realize that what someone else is saying or doing is the result of his unconscious programming.

SUMMARY: UNDERSTANDING PROGRAMS AND PROGRAMMING

Sources of Past Programming

- You accumulated experiences from many sources in many ways, and at different times.
- Learning is sequential and develops through horizontal enrichment and vertical development from sensations, percepts, perceptions, facts, basic understandings and concepts, to generalizations, hypotheses, and theories.
- They result in patterns of feelings, beliefs, and actions physically,

emotionally, socially, and intellectually.

- Your ancestors were programmed themselves, resulting in their perhaps inappropriate behavior, feelings, and beliefs about you.

About Freedom from Inappropriate Programming

- When you know where you came from, where you are now, and where you can go physically, emotionally, socially and intellectually, you can allow your mind and body to climb out of their self imposed jails of programmed thoughts, actions, and feelings.
- You will become much more alert and aware of some of the consequences in your life of programming by yourself and others.
- It eliminates trapped behavior, lack of free will, and the feeling of being a prisoner in a world not of your own making.
- When you learn how to change the process the product will change.
- You can rise to a higher plain–a higher form of functioning and enjoyment as you unravel the threads of your life.
- The process is ongoing and continuous.
- You will be free to determine how you will live the rest of your life.
- You can now find joy and true love–for so many people, places, and things.
- Your new persona will attract others to you.

About Programmed Behavior

- There are many *simple* programs from your past that are operating within you at this very moment. If you had to think about every simple task every time it was performed, you would

have little time for anything else.
- Programs help with *simple* behaviors.
- Many programs from your past and those that you use today are very complicated.
- Programs can conflict with each other.
- You may resent programmed behaviors you have identified in yourself or others.
- You have programs that are unconscious–have not been brought to your awareness or consciousness level.
- Given knowledge of yourself genetically and environmentally (experientially), you can be in charge of the way you view your life.

MORE ABOUT PROGRAMS

- Programs have been learned from birth.
- Programs have different etiologies.
- You may think that programs are of your own making but all are the result of numerous previous internal and external forces.
- Some programs have been imposed upon you–but your programming has permitted it.
- Some programs are a combination of programs imposed upon you and made by you.
- Programs are created from one or more *emotions, beliefs, attitudes and/or behaviors* (EBAB) by you, as the receiver, and as a result of *emotions, beliefs, attitudes and/or behaviors* (EBAB) by others.
- They have one or more *physical, emotional, social and intellectual* (PESI) components.
- Some forces are greater than others in the formulation of programs.
- They have *affects* and *effects* physically, emotionally, socially,

and intellectually in the present.

- You may not be aware of the (PESI) affects of programs on your (EBAB).
- They can be examined rationally through objectively evaluating their genesis.
- Different programs can be considered good or bad.
- They can be appropriate at one time and inappropriate at others.
- They can be examined by exploring their affects and effects on past and present behavior.
- Programs can result in distortions of reality.
- These distortions can affect rational exploration of the etiology and development of other programs.
- Programs are combinations of affects and effects.
- Programs can create different affects and effects.
- Programs have been internalized <u>concretely</u>, *representationally*, and *abstractly*.
- Programs have been learned and reinforced through horizontal enrichment and vertical development.
- Programs can interact with each other.
- One program can take priority depending on the circumstances.
- One program may carry greater (and perhaps irrational, pervasive) strength through time and circumstances.
- It can affect and effect many behaviors.
- It can affect and effect the relative strength of a competing program.
- Programs can reinforce each other.
- Programs can have sequences.
- They have been developed (PESI).
- (PESI) can affect programming.
- Programming and (PESI) can be interactive.

- Programming can affect (PESI) in varying amounts and at varying times.
- Programs can provide stability.
- Some programs are *covert*.
- Outward actions and emotions may not reflect the real programs within a person or group.
- Some programs are *overt*.
- They are the outward expression of felt inner beliefs and emotions.
- Individual programs can be shared with others (PESI).
- Groups have different programs.
- Different group programs can cause comfort, strife, or other feelings, beliefs, attitudes and behaviors to the group and to individuals in the group as well as to those not in the group (PESI) (EBAB).
- Group programs can be ignored, changed, altered, or deleted (PESI) (EBAB).
- Group programs can be shared with others (PESI) (EBAB).
- Recognition of our programming is necessary prior to the change process.
- Rigid programming creates various effects and affects.
- Programs can be valued without being properly evaluated.
- We are often unaware of how programs affect us.
- Activities can reinforce each other.
- Activities can affect redefinitions of a program or programs.
- Activities can serve to eliminate a program or programs.
- One or more programs can take precedence over another program or programs.
- One program can recede into the background. The shift depends on the circumstances.

- You may not realize that much of your life as a result of programming resides in the past or future–very infrequently in the "present."
- You are often unaware of how programs affect you.
- You can become robotic in your feelings, beliefs, and actions.
- (EBAB) by oneself and others precedes development of (EBAB) toward others.
- These (EBAB) in themselves resulted from (EBAB) from the past by oneself and others.
- (EBAB) can affect (PESI).
- Ability to identify and examine programs is affected by level of objectivity.
- Certain programs from the past may make you reject your objective view of other people's actions.
- You may have lost conscious control of your programs and experiences, thereby allowing your life to be programmed by others.

About Program Change

- Programs for change provide change possibilities.
- We can learn to change our programming (PESI) (EBAB).
- Recognition of inappropriate programs functioning within you is necessary before change can take place.
- When you still use past programs and feel uncomfortable, you are ready to change direction.
- By probing your past programs, you can become all that you want to be!
- You may have behaved like everyone else because you did not see alternatives. No one pointed out different ways you could live your life–thinking, feeling, and acting differently from

those around you.

- There are many advantages to changing the ways you look at your feelings, beliefs, and actions.
- You have the opportunity to enjoy the many facets of your life.
- You can function more profitably by a process of redefining your own life and its actions.
- You may not have been aware that so many people were thinking and acting the same way.
- You were not aware that you could do things in your own way, at your own time, and in a place of your choosing.
- When you learn to become a true creator of your own experience, you and everyone you come into contact with will benefit.
- You can attain true freedom (PESI) (EBAB).
- You do not have to be trapped in the box created by programs that were entered into your brain.
- You can learn to recognize and examine the effects and affects of past programming, their impact and their cause/effect relationship.

Results of Past Programming

- Looking at your past can help you recreate, redefine your life today.
- You can learn to recognize that you do not have to repeat the errors you made.
- You need the skills to explore programming's effects and affects on your life today.
- Memories of events that happened many years ago may have resulted in many scenarios that are affecting your life today.
- Inappropriate past programs can create present problems.
- They can prevent your enjoyment of all the good that is around

you today.

- They have many consequences.
- Past programs may still be in charge of your life.
- Maintenance of past programs requires effort.
- Some past programs may appear to give you comfort but they prevent your mind from expanding to its greatest potential.
- Established programs can prevent your living fully in the present (PESI).
- These past behaviors can result in a truly vicious cycle of responding with patterns of behavior that are not viable today.
- These patterns prevent your objective intelligence from examining each scenario from all angles.
- You may be programming those you meet based on past expectations, experiences, or beliefs so that now you expect certain feelings, behaviors, and thoughts from that individual regardless of today's totally different stage.

About Universal Programs

- Society is built on a foundation of beliefs, desires, expectations, and models of how things should be.
- They can be called universal programs because many people function based on programming that the culture or society endorses.
- When reality does not match up with these models, desires and expectations, negative emotions can appear en masse.
- They can manifest themselves in irrational thought and behavior.

The diagram below illustrates how your experiences limit the way you live when you are being directed by your programmed self. You are surrounded by automatic behavior that confines everything about the way you experience life. When you learn to live from your *true conscious self*, your *mindful energy*, you have choices and options that you may not have recognized when you lived from your programmed self. Your experience of life will be more open and filled with a sense of self-direction and freedom.

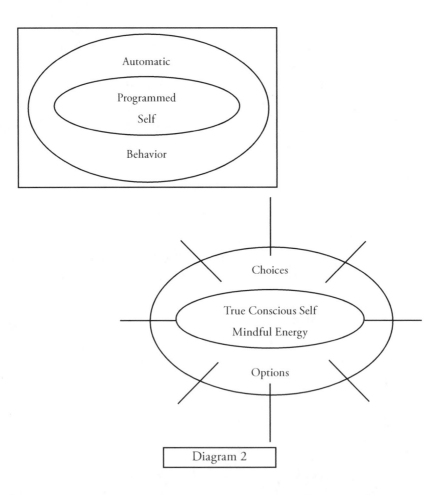

Automatic

Programmed

Self

Behavior

Choices

True Conscious Self
Mindful Energy

Options

Diagram 2

6

PASSIVE MEDITATION AND PRACTICE

You are going to learn that passive meditation is a simple process that allows your mind to rise above the thought level in order to gain critical and fundamental access to a platform from which you can observe (listen to) your thoughts, feelings and emotions. It also acts as a platform to your true self (*mindful energy*). The passive practice of meditation is when you sit quietly, by yourself, without any outer disturbances, such as TV, radio, telephone. You sit with your eyes closed and place all your attention on your natural breathing process. When this passive practice is complete, then give your mind instructions to continue this clarity during your active time.

Are There Different Ways to Meditate?

Yes. I utilize the natural breathing we all do. However, you may use a candle, a sunset, or any focus you choose that is simply an observational focus and not a thought focus. I chose breathing because it is a natural phenomenon, and it is always available to me wherever I go.

What Is the Role of Meditation in Your Daily Life?

Through the medium of the "quiet mind" you can access your *mindful energy* and thereby merge your mind (material aspect) with your pure energy, which is your true essence. As these merge you take on the qualities of your true self and manifest these qualities in your daily life. You will "know" that your life always has been, always is, and always will be perfect for your evolution as a human being in this material dimension.

What Factors Can Prevent and Facilitate the Processes of Active and Passive Meditation?

The so-called "Rational Mind" has been in charge of your life for a long time. It is not prepared to relinquish its dictatorship without a fight. The method it will use is to develop thoughts suggesting the uselessness of meditating. You could be getting things "done" instead of wasting your time meditating. This will be one of those programs that you will delete from your software program.

Your friends and family will look at your meditation practice as being some weird, Eastern practice, which has no value in our present society. Their interpretation of "meditation' is usually not very accurate or well informed.

The basic element that underlies any meditation practice is that the thoughts slow down and allow the clutter in the mind to clear itself out. The re-organization of the thoughts is also basic to meditation. Your *mindful energy* will take over and direct you into the proper path that will enable your maximum development to take place.

What Are Some Effects and Outcomes of Meditation?

Rather than having programmed thoughts determine your feeling and behaviors you can now become the director of your own life's forces. The knowledge you attain through meditation both on a passive and active level can lead you toward your higher essence–your *mindful energy*. You are relieved of the conscious work of thought and you become pure awareness. And yet you are more aware than ever- thoughts are not interfering with your true awareness–your essence of being. You are in a state of all knowingness. You have nothing to fear or worry about. You are perfection. You become so much more aware of how your mind thinks. Things like time, the aging process, where you have been, where you are, where you are going, the swiftness of time passing, the events that have formed your foundations, your ways of thinking and feeling, the ways you move and smell and touch and feel, the ways you integrate your life with those around you, the ways you separate yourself from other, the ways you attach yourself to others, your thoughts about the future, the thoughts that impede your proper functioning, time that has robbed you of your youth, time that stands still in crisis, and time as your enemy.

That's how your rational mind appears to you. But, in fact, what we think of as rational may well be irrational. We delude ourselves into believing that we are being totally objective and honest. You may think that you are aging but you are not your body. Your true essence never ages. Time does not exist for your true essence. It stands still while the illusion of time passes before its eyes.

"Awareness" through meditation is an overseer, observer, and an objective viewer of all that is occurring. Even though it is an overseer it is observing and while observing it is unobtrusively or subtly changing your thought patterns. That's a given. It can also choose to give conscious direction to your thoughts, feelings and actions. When you are aware of what is happening while it is happening you will begin to reach a higher level of being.

Time will appear to expand because of the clarity in your mind. As the clutter dissipates, the mind can have the room to expand and flow effortlessly.

Harmony, peace, and love will prevail and become the focal point of your being. Helping others will become your prime purpose. Your old manufactured self will disappear and your true self will emerge.

The initial objective of passive meditation is to reach your clear space. Your clear space is your mind devoid of thought, while being perfectly aware. A radio can capture radio waves via its internal organization. It uses its channel finder to tune into various channels or different waves of energy. Your mind can also tune into different channels from the clear meditative state from which all channels can be reached. The primary channel is your *"mindful energy"*.

Physical well being, enhanced creativity, and increased energy result. You will control how you experience each moment. Events, situations, what people say or do, environment, etc. will have no effect on you, unless you choose to allow it to do so. You will experience more creativity; more productivity; happiness on a deeper level; enhanced relationships with yourself and others; ability to avoid situations that are not conducive to your health and well being. Knowing that you "know" will give you the confidence to do anything you would like to do.

What Has Meditation Done for Me?

Meditation has enabled me to enter into a clear awareness state from which I can observe my thoughts and programs. I can also tap into my *mindful energy* while in the field. I have learned to enjoy and experience security and peacefulness as I live my life fully aware, at the highest level of my *mindful energy*. My physical energy and the level of my overall health has increased. My relationships are at the highest level ever. I require less sleep. My eye/hand co-ordination in sports activities has been elevated.

What Can Meditation Do for You—What Can You Become Aware of?

If you are walking along and someone hits you on the head you may be rendered unconscious, but you do not realize that you are unconscious until you wake up. Until you can "wake up" from the programming that is running your life you cannot realize that you have been unconsciously programmed or subjected to unconscious programming. When you meditate and transcend the thought level your true essence is evolving.

The author's experience: "I had this awakening myself. As I slept, I found myself going into another dimension: that of consciousness without my physical body. I felt myself going into space. I encountered a huge rubber-like round sphere and entered it. I felt trapped in the sphere and I bounced off the wall when I tried several times to get out. I asked myself: "Well, what is this? Where am I?" I looked down and saw a woman seated at the base of the sphere. I descended to the bottom of this huge sphere, and I had a perception of traveling a long distance. I asked: "Why am I here?" Her response? "To learn." I suddenly felt free to get out of the sphere."

You can look at your body and its place in the world and recognize that you are here to learn. That can be the way you can look at your own experiences. Identify them, observe them, describe them, and think about them. You can use your conscious awareness to recognize what is happening and then feel free to get on with your life in the here and now. You are not trapped in your previous history of pain, remorse or other destructive feelings. You are now in a position to accept what was, and be in a position to accept fully what is, and what you are capable of being.

With regard to answers to life's situations, I have found a more direct channel to obtaining answers. I talk to that mind part of my brain that does the thinking (cerebrum) somewhat as a third party: apart but also still being a very vital element in its functioning. And I can now say: when you have an answer, tell me what to do about it. I do not have the need to proactively prod my mind to "think" about an answer.

What Is the Role of Time in the Process of Meditation?

Time is an asset that is optimized through meditation. It is an asset because you're learning to reach your highest level of being through the medium of time. Your perceptions of time change. Your subjective thinking is sequential(time). "Knowing" is timeless. When you are aware of this, you can then re-evaluate its dimensions and its impact on your life. When you observe without thought, time seems to stand still because you are engaging your timeless self and bringing it into the act. The experience itself is so exciting!

A personal example may shed some light on what we are talking about. When I am actively meditating while walking along the street, I find myself standing still in time. My true essence is standing still. Everything else is revolving around it.

What Do I Do When a Thought Enters My Mind?

Thoughts can enter your mind at any given moment. It is your responsibility to take charge of these thoughts and let them dissolve into nothingness—but being aware of them at the same time through the process of meditation.

When a thought enters your mind, bring your attention back to your breathing. The initial purpose of passive meditation is to constantly focus on breathing. Yes, thoughts may enter your consciousness, but when you concentrate on breathing you can rise to a pure awareness state. This state of awareness is your *mindful energy*, and it allows you to become aware of your true self. *Mindful energy* is both the path and the goal (experiencing your true self.)

Preparation for Meditation

Attitudes Toward Yourself:

- Observing
- Non-judgmental
- Patience
- Open mind
- Trust in yourself
- Non-striving
- Acceptance
- Non-attachment

Attitudes Toward Others:

- Be kind to others
- Help those in need
- Have compassion for others

- Non-judgmental
- Accepting others as they are

Regularity of Necessary Physical Activities:

- Have regular times for toilet, shower, meals, naps, and sleep.

- Organization, Order, and Moderation in All Matters
- Daily Reading of Inspiring Stories of The Sages

Meditation: (Being in the Present on Purpose)

- Meditate daily in the same room and same spot
- Meditative space must be as quiet as possible
- Meditate a minimum of (20) twenty minutes, twice a day. (Once before breakfast and once before dinner.)
- Meditate once a week in the company of others
- Seek no results and expect nothing
- Avoid moods of anger, depression, etc. When you feel a mood entering your consciousness, focus on your breathing and meditate.

What Is the Role of Breathing in the Process?

You train your mind to rise above your thinking process into the pure consciousness level by becoming highly conscious of your breathing. Breathing is usually an ordinary and automatic process, from your autonomic nervous system before birth. But what happens when you get excited or experience a dreadful accident? Your rate of breathing increases and it has effects on all parts of your body.

Correct breathing requires that your stomach slightly RISE and go in front of your body when you are breathing IN, and FALL or sink within your body's cavity when you are breathing OUT! You can readily observe correct breathing when you are lying in a prone position (sleep position). Immediately, stop what you are doing and concentrate on your own breathing pattern. Is it correct? If not, you are not getting sufficient oxygen, and all your body's emotional, physical, social, and intellectual functions are affected negatively. While you are relearning to breathe, or after recognizing that your breathing process is 'correct," you can then focus on observing your own inner state of mind by starting the process of being aware of your breathing. When you begin to observe your breathing and you feel–and see–your stomach rising and falling, you rise above the thought level. (Pure observation automatically allows you to transcend thought).

Your mind is programmed, like that of a computer, and you really "react" to life's situations instead of "choosing to act." When you focus on your breathing, you are "rising above" the thought process, so that eventually you are able to "observe" your own thoughts, which lead to knowing your own programs and then becoming "director" of your programs rather than being the "slave" to your programmed mind.

Passive Meditation Practice

- Find a quiet place, sit or recline. (Do not lie prone).
- Close your eyes and keep your lips closed.
- Focus your awareness on your breath flowing in and out through your nostrils. (Not thinking about your breathing

but being physically aware of the feeling of the breath or your stomach rising and falling).

- Your brain will pick up these new messages and re-organize itself.

Note:
As you breathe in, your stomach should rise up slightly. As you breathe out your stomach goes in slightly.

- When a thought enters your mind, bring your awareness back to your breathing. Sometimes many thoughts will take control of your mind, but eventually you will remember to focus your awareness on your breathing.
- Do not attempt to keep thoughts out of your mind, let every thought flow through.
- The object of meditation is to have no object and no goal. But just to be in the moment by focusing on your breathing. Do not try to force anything to happen.
- Do not try to control your breathing; allow the body to breathe as it will.
- Keep your body as still as possible. If you feel like fidgeting, breathe into the area of your body that feels uncomfortable and feel the relaxation flowing through that part of your body.
- When you become accustomed to the breathing process, you can then start to scan your body starting from your toes and working up to your head. When you feel a part that is tight, breathe into that part until you feel it relax, include all the muscles in your face.
- When you open your eyes after you complete your meditation, open your eyes very slowly.
- Start with ten (10) minutes and build up to forty five (45) minutes,

twice a day. Once before breakfast and once before dinner. If this feels like too much, do whatever feels comfortable to you.

- Eventually you will notice that there are gaps between your thoughts. The thoughts have slowed down and then you may become aware of total awareness without thought. When that occurs, focus on that pure awareness and know that this pure "consciousness" or "awareness" is in reality your true *mindful energy*. You are not your thoughts, your body, and your emotions. You are simply *mindful energy* residing in your present body. In order to experience the "human experience".

- When you finish your "practice" give your mind the suggestion that you will retain this clear mind during your everyday life. Whenever you feel tension or stress of any kind, focus on your breathing with your eyes open. (Active Meditation)

Note 1:

At first you may fall asleep, but this is a natural event because of the release of stress. When you awake, continue the practice.

Note 2:

The mind is programmed, similar to a computer and we usually "Re-act" to life's situations instead of "Choosing to Act." When you focus on your breathing you are "rising above" the thought process, so that eventually you are able to "observe" your own thoughts, which lead to knowing your own programs and then becoming "director" of your programs rather than being the "slave" to your programmed mind. A computer is programmed to do exactly what its software is telling it to do.

Note 3:

Suggested Follow-up: After practice take ten (10) minutes and write down all the thoughts that enter your mind, then read them out loud to yourself with a deep level of awareness.

SUMMARY: UNDERSTANDING MEDITATION AND PRACTICE

Passive meditation is a simple process that allows the mind to rise above the thought level in order to regain control over the so-called "rational mind" in order to attain peace of mind.

"Passive practice" is placing your attention on your breathing, as you sit in a quiet spot.

About Results of the Process of Meditation

- By being in a highly aware intelligent state of mind without any analyzing or thinking, you will simply "know."
- You can choose to retain or let go of certain thoughts over others in your past.
- You can enjoy extra time by not dwelling on unnecessary thoughts, feelings, or actions.
- You will be better able to live your present life fully. You will not be bogged down with all that excess past baggage.
- You will be peaceful within yourself and with the rest of the world.
- Harmony, love and peace will prevail.
- Helping others will become your prime purpose.

To be objective about your life's programming and the thoughts surrounding this programming, you need to get into a meditative zone because it provides you with a platform from which you can observe your thinking. The meditative zone is consciousness without thought.

7

DUAL TRACKING
(ACTIVE MEDITATION)

Dual Tracking is when you apply meditation during all of your daily activities. Active Meditation (Dual Tracking) is when you are engaged in any activity, including eating, bathing, sports, social activities, etc. Your eyes are open and you engage all the normal senses around you as you usually would in those circumstances. However, you are operating on a "Dual Track" which is from a "Quiet Zone" as a background from which you observe all your senses at work. You also observe your "rational mind" doing its thing, thinking. Your vocal system doing its thing, talking. Your limbs are moving, etc. "You know that you know."

"Dual tracking" is a two-part process—doing something and being aware of doing it from the perspective of your *mindful energy*—happening simultaneously. Your clear space, the gap, the pause between stimulus and response allows the wisdom of your *mindful energy* to help you perform at your highest level.

A higher state of awareness takes place through dual tracking. Everything "outer" is viewed by your *mindful energy*, which then integrates its very subtle "knowingness" into the ensuing process. Access to *mindful energy* allows you to experience direct perceptions of truth independent of any reasoning process. This process allows the brain to reorganize itself–how it functions, perceives, and physically reacts. It allows you to be aware of the programming behind your thoughts, actions, reactions, emotions and physical feelings.

New, more appropriate, creative thoughts and actions can now be released into your rational mind. This process cycles continuously in a never-ending spiral promoting your evolution as a human being.

While in the extended universal, all-encompassing zone of *mindful energy*, you are participating in a specific program. During this process, you have the ability to change direction at will–to choose to act rather than react. You are open to the infinite powers of this universal field of awareness where everything is possible. This state of awareness allows the part of your brain that is the center of thinking (the cerebrum) to function in a very creative, free environment. And all you are doing is observing. During the method of observing and brain functioning, the practice of observation is really your higher intelligence entering the process. It becomes integrated with the part of your brain that is thinking. When these two simultaneous forces are functioning maximally, you can then become more analytical and, in turn, more creative as you begin to see so many more possibilities of your higher functioning self (your *mindful energy*) teaching your programmed self.

Eventually, with awareness your rational mind becomes the creative, *mindful energy*.

When Can I Actively Meditate?

You can meditate at any time and in any place. When someone calls you on the phone and is upset about something: focus on your breathing while you are listening. This will help keep you in the objective, aware field where you can respond without feeling emotionally upset yourself. Utilize the time you spend while doing simple everyday things or tasks to reinforce your observational or aware state of mind, i.e., when washing the dishes, feel your hand on the plate, or when taking your dog for a walk, feel your hand on the leash. Meditation is not meant to be solely practiced in a quiet room by yourself. This is only the 'warm-up" period. You then can learn to bring this clear mind into the active portion of your life.

What Is the Overall Sequence in Dual Tracking as it Applies to Your Every Day Life?

Below is the sequence of steps in the process. Specific procedures are included at each step in the process.

- You first meditate in private as a warm-up. This gives you the experience of being perfectly aware with little or no thought in your mind.
- Apply this state of mind to simple everyday tasks. You can apply it to tasks such as washing dishes, drinking water, or brushing your teeth. This enables you to become comfortable with those experiences and bring clarity of mind into your daily life. The experience of peacefulness (non-thought)–simply observing what you are doing. This leads into observing what you are thinking and then evaluation of your actions and your thoughts–then the cause/effect process of all your thoughts and action–you become deliberate.
- Utilize this clarity or state of mind in social situations with your closest ones. While you are with them, step back from them and observe their words, actions, gestures, and interactions with others.

- Use this evolving clarity or state of mind in expanded social activities, physical games, while reading a book. Observe how people act, speak, body language, facial expression, etc. Ask yourself: How conscious are they? Are they just running off their pre-set program? Then look at yourself. Are you doing the same unconscious dance?
- Have an overview while reading a book. Experience your "quiet zone" while you read. At first, you will need to read slower than you usually do, but your reading speed will increase as you practice.

Steps To Get To "Knowing That You Know"

How do I arrive at the "overview" "knowingness" platform? i.e., knowing that you know.

- Passive Meditation: practice focusing your attention on breathing which results in slowing down your river of thoughts. Part of your mind can then transcend your thoughts and "listen" to your thoughts as if listening to a radio program. You can then become objective and the evaluation of thoughts, programs, emotions can take place. Note: during "passive" meditation when a thought arises, you bring your attention back to your breathing, which allows the thought to dissipate without creating conflict. During "active" meditation (dual tracking which is all areas of your daily life outside the "passive" meditation), you can control and manage your mind and its programs to create a peaceful experience.
- In order to train your mind to "actively" meditate, you give a message to your mind for it to remain in this "clear mind"

channel throughout all your activities.

- When you are brushing your teeth, combing your hair, or any other simple task, stand in front of a mirror and look at your reflection as if you are watching a movie. Do not think, but simply observe your physical actions. Note: When you "observe" fully, the mind ceases to think.

- When you are playing golf or tennis, do not think about what you want your body to do. Feel how different parts of your body are moving. At first you will feel each part separately, i.e., hands, feet, shoulders, etc. After some practice, you will be able to "feel" many parts simultaneously.

- When you are walking, pay attention (be aware) of how each foot feels as it touches the ground. No thinking, just pay attention.

- Observe a tree, a bush or a plant. Look at each leaf, or the colors, or the shape of the branches. Simply observe, no thought.

- After you have practiced the physical aspects of observation, you can begin the mental aspects. Take five or ten minutes several times a day. Sit in quiet area with a pad and a pencil, close your eyes, and observe the thoughts as they arise in your mind. Write down each thought as it occurs, exactly as you heard it on your inner radio system. Then read each thought out loud. You then begin to realize these thoughts are not the real you. In many instances, they are irrational. These thoughts are the results of the hidden programs in your mind. Evaluate each thought. Ask the question, "Is this thought of value to me and others?" If not, why not. If not, discard the thought, or re-program the thought. Explore options available to you to replace the inappropriate thought or action.

- After you practice the mental aspect for a while and you become accustomed to 'viewing" your thoughts on paper, you can go on to the next step.

- As you go through your day, be aware of your thoughts as they arise. Evaluate them. Reflect on them. Do not act on them unconsciously. "Choose to act" in lieu of "reacting" with conditioned responses. At first it will seem to be unduly time consuming, but as you continue to practice, it will become second nature.

- As you proceed, you will discover that your inner intelligence will become your friend and ally in all the interactions of life. This life force will guide you into right thought and right actions. You will "know that you know." The "consciousness" you are familiar with now will seem to be more and more "like unconsciousness" as your awareness level increases.

- The end result is that your inner intelligence will operate through this channel of your mind/body machine. This mind/body will seem to do its work in an effortless manner. All your perceptions and goals will change. Materiality will no longer be your goal or your god, but will only serve your true spiritual self. Your thoughts will serve you rather than be your master. Your emotions will remain on a level, constant plane of peacefulness. Your physical body will be healthier and will know what to do to keep its health and energy constant. Your intellectual self will use its powers to aid others and knowledge will be used for the good of others. Regarding social aspects, everyone will be seen as an evolving spirit rather than as their programmed selves. Your over-riding goal will be to evolve into your highest and best self.

- Achieve the ultimate of enjoying life on a moment-to-moment basis without the necessity of programs, and allowing your true self (*mindful energy*) to direct your mind, body, and actions

Practice Mindfulness during All Activity

- When you are engaged in any physical activity–"know what you are doing while you are doing it." I.e. this is the essence of mindfulness practice. For example: when you are walking, "feel" each step as your feet touch the ground. When you drink water, "feel" the water going down your throat.
- Pay attention and see things as they are. There is no need to change anything.
- Realize we only have the "moment" to live
- Know when you are exhaling.
- Know when you are inhaling.
- Say it to yourself: "I know I'm exhaling," etc.
- Bring this knowingness into other automatic daily functions.
- "I know I am raising the glass to my lips."
- "I know I am taking a step forward." etc.
- Touch your knee. Feel your breathing.
- Be consistent. Do it as much as you can on a daily basis. Do it twice or three times a day.

The Goal of Dual Tracking

The purpose of this process is to enable you to function from your true, unbiased self, your core of *mindful energy*.

Through dual tracking–doing and observing at the same time– you can now unlock those higher forces hidden within you. They can be unlocked to free you from the inefficient, unnecessary, repetitive, inappropriate, useless, and biased programs that have held you back from realizing your greatest potential as a human being. Dual tracking enables you to experience other, more optimal ways to live your life. In order to raise your level of consciousness, you have to rise above your automatic action-response level. Use your dual tracking skills to make you more fully aware of that which is going on within and around you. At the same time, you will start to live in the moment. This is an exciting result of this process. This greatly enhances how you experience life.

The chart below looks at the elements that are included when exploring dual tracking.

The Process of Dual Tracking					
Experience	Your Involvement	Role of Clear Space	Effects	Affects	Merging
Thoughts Actions Emotions	Doing and observing simultaneously	Creates platform of awareness to enable rational mind to be directed by *mindful energy*	Mental Physical Emotional Spiritual	Relationships All other aspects of your life	Merging of your *mindful energy* with your rational mind to create your "new personality" which is directed on a continuous basis by your *mindful energy*

PEACEFUL KNOWINGNESS, HIGHER INTELLIGENCE, AND THE ESSENCE OF BEING ALL THAT YOU CAN BE

Peaceful knowingness is a state of mind wherein you are perfectly conscious, aware of everything that is going on within and outside of yourself. You are perfectly accepting of what is in the moment with the knowledge that you are capable of changing the next moment. You can now function at the highest level of your intelligence. You attain your true essence, fulfill your highest potential as a human being. You become the embodiment of your essence.

This Pure Essence (*mindful energy*) created your birth. It is a tiny spark of the intelligence that created and rules the universe as we know it. We are separate from and simultaneously a part of the universal *mindful energy*.

We are all born with potential to be anything and everything human beings can become. In that sense we are all individuals while being a part of the larger whole. For instance, consider opposite character traits of greed and generosity. Each of us is somewhere on that continuum of character, where we are is determined by our programming. However, within each of us is the potential to act out of greed or generosity; totally in one direction or the other. In that sense we are a hologram, participating in a piece of the larger whole while simultaneously encompassing that whole.

Your True Essence of Yourself

Your true essence is attainable in its highest form as you learn how to access its powers. When you have gone through the steps of objective observation, subjective and objective reality, thought, and dual tracking to approach a higher level of awareness, the pure essence of yourself can now come to the fore. You know what is important to know–the essence of your being. This is the beginning of true freedom. You will no longer be a slave to your thoughts, and will become a master of your actions. This is a platform from which we can journey, using the vehicle of pure consciousness, to other dimensions and realities. You truly live each moment because the mind is not "cluttered" by constant thinking, which blurs and changes the "moment." When there is no "clutter," you see clearly. Our usual process is thinking of the past or the future, which takes us out of the present moment. Each moment takes on a life of its own without the interference of the past, or the distraction of the future.

Imagine yourself playing a game of tennis. You can rise above your thought level to a higher consciousness–that of inner intelligence, higher intelligence, and "living in the moment" with complete awareness of what is happening. You rise above yourself, in effect, to become an observer of the feelings, emotions, and actions that are guiding your play. This is a simultaneous occurrence. From this vantage point, you can observe dispassionately from a distance, while being passionate, if you so desire. The alternative higher form of passion emerges, which is the joy of peace of mind. Knowing that all is beautiful and everything that is played out is perfection (past, present and future).

What is the result?

• Your body and mind become "still"
• You know (observe) your play without thought
• Physical action is enhanced
• Intention to release your arm with maximum speed is easily done
• Eye-hand coordination is enhanced
• Speed of movement is enhanced

- Your mind is cleared, allowing your inner intelligence to emerge
- Euphoric joyfulness emerges
- You enjoy the entire game; "winning" or "losing" does not enter into the picture. Neither does playing "well" or "poorly."

Many people are aware only of the external process of "doing things" rather than the whole process that involves getting in touch with their true inner spiritual *mindful energy*. Perfection is being totally aware in each moment which is a clear mind. This is instant gratification. It allows your true *mindful energy* to operate through you. You are a miracle walking, but you don't know it. The way to know it is to allow your mind/body miracle of being to operate itself with "full awareness," while your mind/body is operating. Just relax and watch the show. You will be pleasantly surprised.

You can become your own movie, actor, coach, umpire, director, writer and audience. The clarity emerging within you allows this "surround" reality to exist. You can focus because of the clarity in your mind and body. There is no clutter to fragment its totality. Along with that experience comes enhanced creativity, productivity, peacefulness, better relationships, happiness, and physical and mental health. At last you take charge of your life.

Einstein received his theory of relativity from the quantum field (universal mind which is accessible to all of us through meditation) and then translated it into recognizable form to laymen and the scientific world. I believe we are a microcosm of everything that exists, has existed, and will exist. For example, I believe computers were able to be created because a computer is a reflection of how our own brain/mind operates.

What Happens When You Are in this Place, This Zone, and This State of Being?

You reenergize your mind and body by remaining in this "quiet zone." Being in the zone allows you to create an internal environment to allow perfect balance to occur in body and mind, and enables the body and mind to keep in perfect physical and mental health. You will have more energy and your stress levels will diminish. This will motivate you to continue your practice.

To access the unlimited power, energy, love, and creativity within you, your mind must be cleared of all the debris the ego creates to maintain its existence. The ego's domain lies within security, sensation and power. These are all false gods that you have unknowingly followed in the past.

The source of all energy and/or creation or life force is everywhere, including every atom within your body. Spaces between atoms are the life force that pervades everything. The gap or clear space between atoms is in reality this creative energy or higher intelligence. You have to learn to access the gap for your pure essence to develop most fully.

The Gap is the key unlocking the process: The Hole is the Whole.

The gap, the pause between events internally or externally, is everything. It is timeless, peacefulness, all-knowing, creative, bias-free, objective, repository of everything you are. You are it and it is you. Infinite power, infinite intelligence, infinite energy, everywhere at the same time. The gap is, provides and supports infinite peacefulness.

What Happens When You Are Peaceful?

- Your entire physiology becomes balanced
- Your mental faculties become sharper and your brain is allowed to work at its own pace without any interference from your programs
- The more you access this clear space, the greater capacity you have to enjoy
- Thought is not necessary. You think automatically, however, there is no feeling that you MUST think
- When you reach this clear space in your mind, you approach the essence of life of the entire universe that is within you, as in everything else. You can learn to access it. It is an integral part of your being. You are accessing only a small part of it, but it is a part of the greater whole. The (hole) is the whole. That is, it is the creative energy that has created everything.

How Does This Process Affect You Physically?

On a physical level you will exert less energy and have more mental creativity, and your own mental intelligence system will be balanced at your command. Your immune system will become stronger and more energized. Homeostasis will occur i.e., maintain its stability not withstanding any situation or stimulus.

How Does This Process Affect Sexual Activity?

Once you become proficient in the process of "Dual-Tracking" your mind becomes "still" and you can observe being passionate without thought or expectations interfering.

You can prolong your sexual activity, perhaps indefinitely, because of the control you have on your thoughts and physical self.

Your focus is on just "being" which brings forth the qualities of your true self, one of which is caring for the "other" rather than yourself. This translates into your partner caring for you. The result is "holistic euphoria".

Since "non-thought" or "beingness" brings the body into perfect balance all the physical mechanisms operate optimally.

You can relax completely, watch the show, and be your own director. You remain in the "moment", where time ceases to exist.

One of the reasons, if not the primary reason humans enjoy sex is because they lose their ego selves in the act. There is no thought going on, which is new and exhilarating for most people. If you start with "no thought" you are ahead of the game.

How Does This Process Affect You Mentally–or Intellectually?

On a mental level, your thoughts will be clarified and become more incisive. Freedom from previous inappropriate programs allow you to exhibit more creativity, more perception, fully developed objective, unhampered, and unimpeded awareness. With increased clarity, you avoid assumptions. Rather, you examine everything "in the present" to attain your fullest recognition of its (your thoughts) operation. Your internal operation is viewing the "present" objectively and choosing the best option for your progress.

How Does This Process Affect You Emotionally?

On an emotional level, you will be peaceful, have more tolerance, and be less judgmental towards other people. You will not harbor past inappropriate emotions. You will accept what was, and put your past behind you. When an inappropriate emotion rises within you, concentrate on your breathing (see Meditation Practice). This allows your emotion's negative effects to dissipate, clearing your mind toward reaching an inner harmony of all factors in your life. Your orchestra is now superbly playing your own composition. All of your being blends into your new existence, freed from past emotional missteps.

How Does This Process Affect Your Relationships? Your Evaluation of Others Actions?

You will realize other people are the slaves to their thoughts and "know not what they do." You understand their actions are based on their programs, and in reality have nothing to do with you. You are either in the wrong place at the wrong time, or you are supposed to be there to benefit both of you with lessons learned.

You will become attuned to events, feelings, and behaviors as they happen and you will be able to apply your new skills of objective observation through dual tracking to be in the "aware state" and be in the moment simultaneously. This process will reinforce your reorganizing process and the speed at which the higher intelligence that you possess can take over the "director's" role in your life as you interact in society. You will become tolerant to other people's inappropriate thoughts and actions. They will realize on a deep level that you are understanding and non-judgmental.

A Higher Level of Consciousness

We have delved into selected parts of daily life to understand relationships better, play the game more effectively, act, feel, and think more objectively and responsibly toward ourselves and the rest of society. These newly discovered skills must be worked on daily. You will find that they will result in better business behavior and personal happiness. As you find your own purpose in life, you will increase your charitable giving, teach others the joys of your discoveries, and savor their rewards of better health.

About Your Mindful Energy

- Reaching your *mindful energy* allows you to live fully in the present physically, emotionally, socially, and intellectually.
- Attaining your *mindful energy* is achieved by complete, constant living in the present. It requires certain understandings and constant effort.
- People's behaviors may not be directed to you personally, but may be *reflections of their own programs.*
- You do not have to be affected negatively by them.
- You do not have to let past programming of yourself and others affect your life today.
- You can learn from your past history.
- You can have compassion for those who may have acted unwisely.
- On a universal level, you can change the way people use their minds.
- You can rise to this level of *mindful energy.*

- Many roads lead to attainment of your *mindful energy.*
- You can learn specific techniques.
- They can guide you to a high level of awareness.
- You can learn to attain your *mindful energy* or highest state of mind.
- Visualization is a part of this process.
- Meditation is a part of this process–active and passive.
- A higher level of awareness can also be called your *mindful energy.*
- Your inner essence or your higher being.
- You entered life as a clean plate with nothing on it–no good, no bad.
- You can attain your true essence–your higher intelligence through dual tracking.

What Are Your Ultimate Goals?

- Look at the following checklist at least every day–preferable even more! Remind yourself to rise above your actions, feelings, and beliefs to:
- Be the best that you can be.
- Have sensitivity in every situation.
- Transform yourself into your own new model of being human.
- Recognize and act on transforming your outer form to reach true innerperfection.
- Live in a state of happiness and joy.
- Have faith and confidence in yourself. Allow the knowledge that already exists within your mind, and allow your mind to do what it does best.

- Take charge.
- Become the author, writer, director, producer, and audience of your own life's play.

It does not make sense to allow something that has already occurred to cause you distress. You can't change it, that page has turned. Rather use your energy to learn from the situation, and to handle the effects in lieu of being unhappy, which is of no value to anyone. Why not "choose to act" instead of "re-acting?" Why not choose to be calm and peaceful instead of conflicted and unhappy? You do not have to fall into the trap of acting in your usual, programmed way. Do not let yourself get in the position of not realizing what is happening. Do not take it for granted that because most everyone acts this way there is no other way. Recognize and deal with your irrational thoughts and intense and wasteful emotions.

Practical Effects of Staying in This Clear State of Mind.

You evolve into the highest form of humanity by tuning into higher forms of knowledge and intelligence that exist in the quantum (all knowing, universal mind) dimension. Remember that you have options. The only unchanging constant in your life is your *mindful energy* (your true self). Everything else is always changing including your thoughts, physical bodies, weather, world events, etc.

Why not stay connected to this "constant self"? You will be anchored and secure from ill winds of change. You are immortal. These bodies are only temporary vehicles you use to experience this dimension. You can see things clearly and enjoy the constant change without becoming emotionally involved. A new kind of peaceful/joy arises from the true essence of your being which is love in its true form–not physical or emotional–a contentedness beyond the thought level, coming from the cellular level from which you evolved. The starting point was the sub-atomic level, the energy before material existed–the energy from which you were created.

SUMMARY: DUAL TRACKING

Dual Tracking is doing something and being "aware" of doing it, happening simultaneously . You are "aware" of doing it from the level of your *mindful energy*. This means that you "know that you know".

The first level of knowing is from the perspective of your five senses. The next level is from the perspective of your *mindful energy* (knowing that you know).

The following becomes available to you through the process of Dual Tracking:

- Awareness of your own programming.
- Direct perceptions of truth independent of any reasoning process.
- New, creative thoughts and actions are released into your rational mind.
- Becoming open to the infinite powers of the universal field of awareness where everything is possible.
- Capability of functioning from your true unbiased self at the highest level of your intelligence.
- Clarity of mind in all situations.
- The experience of peacefulness and subsequent absence of stress.
- Ability to choose to act rather than re-act

- True freedom from your thoughts
- Master of your actions
- Instant gratification
- More energy
- Perfect health
- Holistic sexual enjoyment
- Mental clarity
- Emotional balance
- Understanding relationships

8

THE ENTIRE PROCESS AND YOUR NEW PERSONALITY

The entire process is comprised of many elements. The following is a review of these elements.

CONSCIOUSNESS is the envelope within which all of our life thoughts and experiences occur. There are four levels of consciousness:

- Waking
- Sleeping
- Dreaming
- Knowing (*mindful energy*)

Few of us have accessed the Fourth level. Meditation can give you access to this Fourth level.

This all important fourth level will guide us to the realization of who we really are. We have been missing the point of who we are and why we are here. Being in the Fourth level may answer these questions for you.

EXPERIENCE differs from consciousness because it requires action. To experience something requires active participation. There are many ways to experience what is going on in your life and in the lives of others. We are capable of choosing exactly how we experience the events of our lives. The level at which we experience our lives can have a profound effect on our health, happiness, creativity, peacefulness and overall outlook on life. However, we have unconsciously relinquished control of how we experience life and most of us are at the mercy of our hidden programs, which dictate each and every one of our experiences.

THOUGHT is the medium through which we live our lives. However, we rarely think about this thought process and how it directs our lives and the experience of our lives. Thoughts usually "think" us (like the tail wagging the dog). We can learn to become director of our thoughts and enhance every aspect of our experience. We can realize that thoughts are not who we really are.

PROGRAMS AND PROGRAMMING are the "software" of our Bio-computer (analogy of a mechanical computer to the biological computer of a human being). The accumulated residual effects of our experience resulted in patterns of behavior, which I choose to call programs. These programs dictate our behavior, actions and reactions to everyone and everything in our environment. We need to identify and explore our present programming in order to objectively evaluate the impact of past programming on our lives today.

By doing so we can choose to keep those aspects that enhance our lives and discard those which hamper our development into evolved human beings.

PASSIVE MEDITATION is the initial process that enables us to "get out of the box" in order to observe our thoughts and programs. We can then become master of our thoughts and programs. We can then pro-actively choose our minute to minute experience of our lives.

DUAL TRACKING (ACTIVE MEDITATION) is a two part process—doing something and being aware of doing it from the perspective of your *mindful energy*. All this happens simultaneously. The wisdom of your *mindful energy* enables you to perform at your highest level of intelligence. You will recognize your ego-self and your true self during your activities. The purpose of this process is to enable you to function from your true, unbiased self.

Your New Personality. The results of all of the above will be your new personality. Mindful energy will emerge as your true self. Life becomes enjoyable and effortless, no matter what the situation happens to be. You handle everything with ease and equanimity.

SUMMARY: THE ENTIRE PROCESS

About Living in the Present

- You are now the embodiment of your entire past.
- Knowledge of your past helps to explain your present.
- Behaviors by others may be misinterpreted.
- Living in the present requires certain understandings.
- To live in the present is not to deliberately delete the past.
- It requires a process of constant effort.
- You may have allowed outside events and people to create your experience of life.
- You may have become robotic in your thinking and emoting.
- You can evaluate your impact on their life.
- You can evaluate their impact on you.
- You can learn to modify your life. Living in the present is the goal of examining and probing your life's feelings, beliefs, and actions.
- Living in the present has many advantages.
- You are unencumbered by past inappropriate programming.

You can function and be happiest by both being a part of, and apart from, the reality of the moment.

When you are experiencing life from your programmed self, most of your thinking is done on the rational, cognitive level. As you read the book and practice the exercises and meditation, your mind will move toward *pure awareness* in addition to rational, cognitive thought. The more often you practice the skills that you are learning, the greater will be your ability to know your *true conscious self* and the *mindful energy* that will enable you to direct the experience of your life.

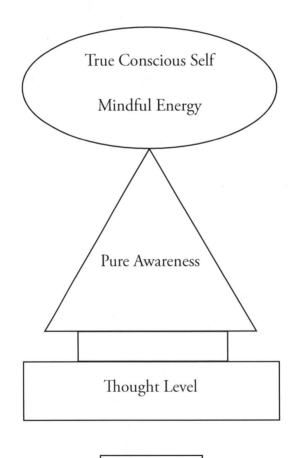

Diagram 3

YOUR "NEW" PERSONALITY

The new personality observes and allows its *mindful energy* to take over. It is effortless. Difficult situations do not exist because they were only illusions after all (a product of our programmed filter system).

When you rise above your thought level into a pure awareness state, you become director of your thoughts; you become conscious! But few have experienced pure awareness without thought. You can discover that everything that you do becomes the optimum you can do at that moment. (See the following explanation of your new personality.) You can make "awareness," which is your true nature, emerge to the forefront. Your egoistic self may be diminished as you begin to realize that it is detrimental, extraneous, wasteful of all your potential energies and inappropriate to your rise to enlightenment. Its value is at best, questionable.

The entire process allows you to become whole. Everything changes and you emerge to become an entirely new entity. In effect you have metamorphosed to become your own new creation. As you emerge from inappropriate past behavior to the true essence of yourself, you will recognize that this change and its rewards are also available to everyone, provided that he knows about it. Share your insights with others, as the whole process becomes a totally new alphabet. You are better able to read messages from within yourself and from others in totally new ways to foster growth of energies you never knew existed. When you learn to see clearly you can understand that other people's actions are governed by their own programs and their interpretations of reality. They are not to blame for their actions. They are primarily on "automatic pilot". But you have now risen above this level of functioning. Take advantage of it and work on it constantly.

Opt out of your current thinking to recognize that you don't really have a past or future–just the present. The only real thing we have is the present moment. Using this process you can achieve "Instant Gratification" every moment of every day.

Now is the time to determine which thoughts are programmed and which are spontaneously created from your true self.

When you have resolved these questions in your mind the answers will allow you to recognize that you can "be" by coming from your inner directorship rather than from previous programming. Before, programming had complete control. Now you have control. Inner intelligence, your *mindful energy* has become the controller or director of your entire being.

Until you can stay connected with your true self you will always be at the mercy of outer change and your inner programs that constantly interpret life and lead you to the yo-yo experience of happiness–sorrow. But when all the doors reopen and infinite peace, energy, intelligence, is allowed to flow through, your self is regenerated. Act from your true self and not your programmed self. Think the same way.

When you learn to see clearly, you can understand that other people's actions are governed by their own programs and their interpretations of reality. They are not to blame for their actions. They are primarily on "automatic pilot." But you have now risen above this level of functioning.

Physically:

Hand eye coordination improves significantly. Movement is fluid. Energy level increases and remains constant throughout the day.

There is a feeling of well being and re-generation occurring in every cell of the body.

Intellectually:

Your thoughts are more positive. There are fewer thoughts, but the thoughts that do appear are peaceful, loving, understanding, non-judgmental. Everything just "is" (i.e. more objective) less emotional. I have a feeling that everything I need to know will come to me. The result of being "quiet" is to allow the proper thinking to come through the "door." The learning curve seems to shrink as "knowingness" takes over. Knowledge of a different level appears on a very subtle level, as if I already know everything that is important.

Emotionally:

The yo-yo effect of being 'sad" and being "happy" smoothes into a straight line. There is only the medium of peacefulness and knowingness. When the mind is clear, everything just "is." There is no running toward or grasping for the carrot of happiness. Happiness is, was, always will be, as long as we can live in the clarity of the mind, i.e., no constant clutter and baggage which our programs create.

Social Aspects:

Since judgment no longer exists, I realize clearly that the mind/body structures we live in are not really who we are. Therefore, I look beyond the structure and what I find is "me" looking back at myself. With that mind set, it is quite easy to relate to everyone, have compassion for everyone, understand everyone, like everyone, etc. Other people realize this on a deeper level, and they respond accordingly.

The usual robot-like reactions and speech are gone. Replaced by a deeper knowingness that chooses the appropriate speech, tone of voice, body language, and real response–ability.(The ability to respond at your highest level) This happens fluidly, not pre-conceived. It is all quite spontaneous and interesting to observe.

Goals:

My goals are humanistic. Material goals seem unimportant except to foster the humanistic goals. It is all about being truly "conscious" and knowing" as much as possible. It is about evolving and refining my body/mind/soul to the highest degree possible. It is about sharing all I have learned with other people in a manner in which they can understand. "Difficult situations" cease to exist because of this clarity of mind. Each situation is just another situation.

Feelings:

Floating through the river of life, as if I were a leaf taken every which way by the swirling current of life. Looking at the ever-changing scene, events, people, interactions, my own growth, other people's growth or lack of it. Quietness, peacefulness, knowingness.

Operational:

Allowing my real self–higher intelligence, to operate me. Having faith in knowing that whatever is happening in my life is what is supposed to happen. All for a purpose I only partially understand. Looking at each situation from many aspects including the reference point and perspective of the other people involved. Being aware of the physical aspects such as my diet, exercise, mental habits, programs, etc. with the view of improving all of the above. Not in a hurried, anxious manner, but in a knowing, feeling manner.

Why it Does What it Does

It only does because it feels right from every point of view. It comes from your deeper self where there is no "why" but only truth, love, understanding, evolvement.

What it Does Not Do

No anger, no conflict, no judgment, no expectations.

Assets and Rewards

My chief reward is instant gratification, simply "to be" in each moment. Everything flows from this central point.
  In addition:

- Greater creativity
- Greater productivity

- Greater efficiency
- Better health–physically and mentally
- Greater skill in sports activities
- Enhanced social relationships
- Enhanced peacefulness
- Elimination of conflicts
- Greater understanding of others
- Greater compassion for others
- Business effectiveness and success

About Taking Charge

- You can take charge of your life.
- You may not be aware of how you can do this.
- You can learn how to take charge of your life.
- You can know what you are thinking, feeling and doing at all times.
- Knowing how thoughts, feelings and sensations arise is prerequisite to taking charge of your life.
- You can learn to evaluate positive and negative impacts of your thoughts, feelings, and actions on your life.
- You can make the determination that now is the time to begin your personal process of renewal and growth.
- You can carry through this process of change to all of your life's experiences.
- You may be able to change the lives of those around you.
- You will be able to make better choices.
- You will function better by developing more appropriate programs to enjoy life to the fullest.

About Conflicts

- Conflicts may have arisen because of opposing forces that have accumulated over the years.
- They may have arisen because of mixed signals from within you and others.
- You may be operating inappropriately because of them.
- You may not even be aware of their operating within you at this very moment.
- They may now be directing your life (PESI and EBAB-see Glossary).
- Present feelings, actions, and thoughts based on past inappropriate programming are wasteful and unproductive.
- If internal changes do not take place, you will not be able to attain the highest levels of self-fulfillment that you are capable of and desire.

About Being Comfortable and Comfort Levels

- "Comfort level" can promote or deter changes in programs
- Being comfortable can be a manifestation of boredom, repetitive action and reaction.
- It can go on for years when you do not recognize other possibilities.
- You may be passing by many excitements of life.
- You have to examine your behavior and your feelings before you can really accept yourself as being comfortable.
- Only then can you evaluate its restraints or possibilities.
- You may not be aware of your behavior, feelings, and attitudes

every moment of each day and for longer periods of time.
- Much of what you do and say is automatic.
- These scenarios can carry over into more important aspects of your life.
- You do not think of the consequences of your feelings or actions and even they become automatic. You have programmed yourself to be comfortable but you may not be aware of at what level you are functioning.
- Change can take place when you realize that your comfort level may not be getting you anywhere.
- You may have bad feelings as you live your daily life, but, surprisingly, they can be comfortable! You may continue thinking the same thoughts, feeling the way you do, and behaving the way you do despite your negative feelings.
- When you realize the feeling of being uncomfortable, you can begin the process of change.

About the Process of Change

- There are well-defined steps in the process of change.
- Identify the source of your feeling, thought, or action.
- Look at it objectively as you explore its etiology physically, emotionally, socially, and intellectually.
- Evaluate its strength.
- Determine its relevance, value, or necessity in your life today.
- Determine what effect it is having on your today in all areas of your living.
- Pick those that are of value to you.

CONCLUSION

"INSTANT GRATIFICATION"

You have been introduced to a process to help you regain your true nature, which is simply *mindful energy* not blocked by the spins (interpretations) of the ego-driven thoughts that were created by the programs that now seem so inappropriate and self-defeating. But be careful. Recognize that many of your interpretations are guided by programs that were imprinted on your "software" ever since you were born. These programs generated waves of thought that were similar to the waves on a lake or pond. These waves distorted reality. But reality just "is." You create a spin on "what is" to create your own version of reality. There is an area between the clarity of the spirit (intelligent, all-knowing, loving) and external events. This area is occupied by your programmed filters, which create the "stirrings" of your brain. Part of this is governed by your ego, which really is another series of programs you have learned. If you can think and simultaneously be in contact with or actually be your *mindful energy*, then the programs will dissolve or be seen for what they are. They are illusions you created yourself to interpret what is happening. At first glance your programs may appear to be so comfortable and easy to live with that they prevent discovery of potential disruption of your own complacency. But the reflections of the sky, trees, and birds, in the water are only that–reflections. They are distorted by the waves on the water. They are not seen for what they really are. If the water is your spirit, you can now recognize that ripples (things that impinge upon you internally or externally) can affect your life. Distortions can take place, and inappropriate feelings, behaviors, and thoughts may emerge. When an event occurs, your programs generate your own interpretation of what that event means to you. That interpretation may include bad judgment, intolerance, anger, frustration, etc. Or, based on your newly discovered ability to examine these events, you may then begin to put them in proper perspective so that they can enrich your life daily and in the long run. In effect, you can reprogram yourself to benefit, rather than be destroyed, dismayed, or confused by those events. In that way, you will benefit most from your newly found method of operating optimally within your new fully objective, observant state of mind.

Be an active participant in your own life. Keep asking the question: "Is this thought, feeling, or action of value to me and to everyone around me?" Then write your own answer to this question.

WHAT ARE YOUR RESPONSIBILITIES AS YOU PROCEED?

Your explorations will become much more satisfying as you learn to be more objective. You will be better able to reach logical conclusions. You will be able to examine critically everything that you see, do, read, and hear about so that you will not fall into the traps so many others do: carrying rumors with them as "truths," spreading false information as "fact," and giving their opinions as though they were based on really objective observation.

But above all, you have responsibilities to yourself. Your primary goal is to "wake up", observe and access your mindful energy, which in reality is your "true self" inhabiting this vehicle of mind/body. This process allows you to "take charge" of your life. This new level allows you access to the master program of holistic living, which is to operate from a peaceful, non-judgmental, harmonious space and which will be the foundation for all your rational mind programs; this is self-realization.

GLOSSARY

AWARENESS: Consciousness

BEHAVIORAL Objective: A clear description of your educational expectations for students when written in behavioral terms and objective; it will include three components: student behavior, conditions of performance, and performance criteria.

BEING: the state of mind in which you experience the complete or perfect state of absolute existence, without the necessity of needing or desiring anything else.

BIO-COMPUTER: Analogy of a mechanical computer to the biological computer of a human being.

BOX: an enclosure consisting of one's mental programs in the mind (i.e. through which all objective reality pass through prior to becoming one's experience), which allows one only to perceive reality within the confines of these programs.

COMMUNICATION: The exchange of information, symbols, or messages through human and media methods.

DUAL Tracking: being spiritual and allowing your brain to function simultaneously. Doing something and being aware of doing it from the perspective of your *mindful energy.* Observing oneself operating itself, including operation of mental activity or physical activity; a sense of being outside yourself during all of your activities while simultaneously being the director of all your activities. Directing from your *mindful energy* rather than your ego-self.

EBAB: Emotions, beliefs, attitudes, and behavior.

EGO: The "I" or self of any person that is programmed by security, sensation, power, greed, and self-interest.

ESSENCE: The basic, real, and unvariable nature of a thing or person or its significant individual feature or features, especially a spiritual or immaterial entity.

EXPERIENTIALLY: Pertaining to or derived from experience, rather than thinking about it.

GAP (The): Pure awareness or knowingness. The space between thoughts.

GENIUS: When someone can do what others need to learn how to do.

HOLISTIC: The theory that whole entities, as fundamental components of reality, have an existence other than is the mere sum of their parts, i.e. mental, physical, and spiritual as a whole can define one's true self only if they are acting together as one unit with the mental and physical actions emanating from the spiritual part which unifies all parts.

Homeostasis: The tendency of the physiological system to maintain eternal stability owing to the coordinated response of its parts to any situation or stimulus tending to disturb its normal condition or function.

Intelligent Awareness: The form of awareness in which one is conscious of perceiving and being aware. A skill developed through this program to monitor one's thoughts, feelings, and actions i.e. knowing that you know.

Internalize Abstractly: To make part of oneself through an idea or concept.

Internalize Concretely: To make part of oneself through actual experiences rather than abstractions; having an actual or existent experience as one's reference.

Internalize Representationally: To make part of oneself through visualization or image.

Internal Programming: Mental programs that you have unconsciously adopted from your parents, teachers, friends, the media, etc.

Knowing: Awareness that you are observing your thoughts (listening), emotions (feelings), and actions (watching), as example: if you were watching a movie and being aware you are watching a movie, without identifying with the characters in the movie.

Knowing that You Know (*mindful energy*): A sense of being outside yourself and observing your conditional (act or process of knowing, i.e. perception) actions as they are happening. This is a simultaneous occurrence.

KNOWINGNESS (Pure Awareness): Pure consciousness with no thoughts (the Gap between thoughts).

MEDITATION: A simple process that allows your mind to transcend (rise above) the thought level in order to gain access to that area of the mind from which you can observe (listen to) your thoughts, feelings and emotions, or be in that area in an aware state with no thought, feeling or emotion.

METAMORPHOSIS: A complete change of identification from your ego-oriented self to your true self of *mindful energy.*.

MIND: The thinking and perceiving part of consciousness, the seat of one's total experience of the psyche and the external environment.

MINDFUL Energy: direct perception of truth independent of any reasoning process. The life force residing within each person. This force is loving, compassionate, caring, powerful and knowing, moral, ethical, non-judgmental, altruistic core of pure energy that contains the intelligence of the universe. The more time you can spend communicating with this life force, the more peaceful and aware you will become. The ability to have the direct perception of truth independent of any reasoning process will be enhanced. The sixth sense enabling you to access the fourth dimension. (Knowing that you know).

OBJECTIVE Aware Field: The level of awareness in which one has the ability to consciously discriminate, evaluate, and refine one's cultural and personal programs and monitor one's own thoughts.

OBJECTIVE Reality: The quality of knowing or perceiving objects, real and actual, distinguishable from thoughts existing only in one's mind.

Objectivity: The ability to know and to understand apart from one's subjective and personal thinking and feeling.

Observation: Perception or notice of internal and external phenomena and objects. For the purposes of this program it defines observation as perception without evaluation or thought, from the perspective of the rational mind.

Persona: The public personality; the mask or façade presented to satisfy the demands of the situation or the environment and not representing the inner personality of the individual.

PESI: Physical, emotional, social, intellectual.

Programming, Program, Re-Programming: Patterns of behavior. Habitual mental habits of behavior, filters in the mind through which all objective reality pass through prior to becoming one's experience.

Pure Awareness (Knowingness): A conscious, alert, knowing state of mind without thought, feeling or emotions.

Pure Consciousness: Being fully awake with no thoughts (being aware that you are fully awake with no thoughts). Pure consciousness exists all the time but we are usually not aware of its existence.

Reality: The quality or fact of being actual, true, and having objective existence.

Residuals: The programming that remains to discomfort or disable a person when certain situations arise that bring up this old programming.

Robotic (automatic): A person who acts and responds in a mechanical, routine manner, usually subject to another's will. In this book, the will we are subject to is our own mental programs.

Self: A person referred to with respect to complete individuality. Can be viewed as the self identifying with one's ego, or identifying with one's *mindful energy.*

Software (programs): The habitual mental programs present in one's brain from which all subjective experience is created.

Spiritual: Wholeness or being in a very still, non-thinking state of mind; nothing fragmented. i.e., *mindful energy*

Subjective Reality: The reality existing in one's own mind, and created by all the programs and perceptions of ones own mind, rather than to the object of thought. Includes personal feelings, prejudice, or programming, biased; personal.

State of Mind: The condition the mind is in as we operate on a minute-to-minute basis. For example: ego state or *mindful energy* state.

Thought (Levels of Thought): Products of thinking, a notion, an idea.

True Self: One's essential being that is informed through *mindful energy,* and is *mindful energy.*

Universal Mind: The spiritual source of life, substance, and intelligence.

Wholeness: A sense or quality of completeness, unity, and integration especially pertinent for the connection between the mind, body, intellect, emotions, and spiritual self.

Zone: State of intensely focused perception to the exclusion of all internal and external stimuli.

SELECTIVE BIBLIOGRAPHY

I recommend the following books, all of which entered into my own education:

Bach, Richard. *Jonathan Livingston Seagull*. New York: Avon Books, 1970.

Chopra, Deepak M.D. *Quantum Healing*. New York: Bantam Books, 1989.

Das, Lama Surya. *Awakening the Buddha Within*. New York, NY: Broadway, 1997.

Goldstein, Joseph. *Insight Meditation: The Practice of Freedom*. Boston, MA: Shambhala Publication, 1993.

Hart, William. *Vipassana Meditation as Taught by S.N. Geonka*. San Francisco, CA: Harper Collins Publishers, 1987.

Holmes, Ernest. *The Science of Mind*. New York: Dodd, Mead and Company, 1938.

Keyes, Ken Jr. *Handbook to Higher Consciousness.* St. Mary Kentucky: Love Line Books, 1975.

Kabat-Zinn, Jon. *Full Catastrophe Living.* New York: Dell Publishing, 1990.

Whereever You Go, There You Are.

Kornfield, John. *A Path with Heart.* New York, NY: Bantam, 1993

Krishnamurti, J. *Exploration into Insight.* San Francisco: Harper and Row Publishers, 1979.

Levine, Stephen. *A Gradual Awakening.* New York: Doubleday, 1979

Nhat Hanh, Thich. (Ed. By Arnold Katler) *The Path of Mindfulness in Everyday Life.* New York, N. Y. Bantam Books, 1991.

Nhat Hanh, Thich. *Peace is Every Step.* New York: Bantam Books, 1991.

Odier, Daniel. *Nirvana Tao.* London: East West Publication (UK), 1974.

Ram Dass. *Grist for the Mill.* Santa Cruz, CA: Unity Press, 1976.

Steiner, Rudolf. *Knowledge of the Higher Worlds and its Attainment.* New York: Anthroposophic Press Inc., 1947.

Swami Prabhupāda, A.C. Bhaktivedanta. *Bhagavad-Gita as it is.* California: The Bhaktivedanta Book Trust, 1968, 1972.

Suzuki, Shunryu. *Zen Mind, Beginners Mind.* New York: Weatherhill Inc., 1970.

Trungpa, Chogyam (ed. By Carolyn Rose Gisnian) *Shambala and The Sacred Path of the Warrior.* Boston, MA: 1988